WONDERS OF MAN

THE WHITE HOUSE

by Kenneth W. Leish

and the Editors
of the Newsweek Book Division

NEWSWEEK, New York

NEWSWEEK BOOK DIVISION

JOSEPH L. GARDNER *Editor*

Janet Czarnetzki *Art Director*

Edwin D. Bayrd, Jr. *Associate Editor*
Laurie P. Phillips *Picture Editor*
Eva Galan *Assistant Editor*
Kathleen Berger *Copy Editor*
Susan Storer *Picture Researcher*
Russell Ash *European Correspondent*

S. ARTHUR DEMBNER *Publisher*

WONDERS OF MAN

MILTON GENDEL *Consulting Editor*

Chester Prosinski *Designer, The White House*

Grateful acknowledgment is made for permission to
quote from the following: to Harcourt Brace Jovanovich,
Affectionately, F.D.R., by James Roosevelt and Sidney
Shalett, copyright © 1959 by James Roosevelt and Sidney
Shalett (pages 154–55); to Charles Scribner's Sons, *Letters to Kermit from Theodore Roosevelt*, edited by Will
Irwin, copyright © 1946 by Charles Scribner's Sons
(pages 83 and 146–47) and *Theodore Roosevelt's Letters
to His Children*, edited by Joseph Bucklin Bishop, copyright © 1919 by Charles Scribner's Sons, renewal copyright © 1947 by Edith Carow Roosevelt (pages 82, 83,
86, and 91).

Endpapers:
*In this highly romanticized engraving of 1839, the
White House appears as a gleaming palace set in a
sylvan glade. Tiber Creek, the southern boundary of
the grounds, was filled in the 1880's and its course
covered over by Constitution Avenue.*
Right:
*This bronze-doré candelabrum, bought for the
White House by President Monroe in 1817, today
decorates a mantelpiece in the East Room.*
Page 12:
*Flags of the President and of the United States flank
the entrance to the Blue Room on the first floor.
Above the door is the presidential seal.*

Contents

An 1848 engraving shows the White House on a quiet day during the Polk Presidency. The statue of Jefferson now stands in the Capitol rotunda.

Introduction

The most imposing address in the United States is 1600 Pennsylvania Avenue, Washington, D.C. It belongs, of course, to the White House, official home of the President since 1800. As an architectural statement or an engineering accomplishment, the building is entirely unexceptional. What makes it unique — especially in the bipolar world that has developed since the end of World War II and especially with the growing importance of the Executive in the American political scheme — is the enormous power that lies within the grasp of its principal resident. That power travels with the Chief Executive, and the words "The White House" now stand for the office of the Presidency — wherever the incumbent may be traveling — as well as for the handsome structure in the nation's capital.

Yet the White House is far more than a symbol of sovereignty; it is the home of a man and his family — a home often mercilessly exposed to the curious though not unfriendly gaze of the republic's citizens, but a home nonetheless. Within its walls, in addition to the great dramas of state, have been enacted scenes of domestic happiness and personal tragedy. In the prescribed and familiar round, weddings, births, deaths have taken place as presidents and their first ladies have seen children born, grow, get married themselves, or sometimes die young. For some families — notably the Theodore Roosevelts — dwelling at the pinnacle of American society was an unalloyed joy; for a number of first ladies — including Letitia Tyler, Carrie Harrison, Ida McKinley, Helen Taft, and Ellen Wilson — the White House years ended in death or incapacitating illness. Eight chief executives have died in office, their coffins traditionally displayed to a mourning public in the elegant and somber East Room.

Nearly every family that has lived in the Executive Mansion has left some mark on the nation's principal residence — from the John Adams inscription carved on a mantelpiece in the State Dining Room to the recent redecoration of the Red, Green, and Blue rooms by Patricia Nixon. The Monroes selected the exquisite bronze-doré table decorations that are an adornment of state dinners; the china collection represents every past President. Theodore Roosevelt and Harry S. Truman oversaw extensive renovations of the structure itself. Grace Coolidge and Mamie Eisenhower acquired antiques for the interior, a custom that reached a triumphant climax with the restoration undertaken by Jacqueline Kennedy.

Most of the White House — the office wings and the upper floors — are closed to the general public. But for the 1,500,000 people who tour the public rooms on the first floor each year, a visit to the White House provides a warm and exciting review of the American past.

THE EDITORS

THE WHITE HOUSE IN HISTORY

I

The President's Palace

George Washington and Pierre Charles L'Enfant shared a vision. The venerated first President of the United States and the brilliant but quixotic French architect both dreamed that a great and beautiful city would rise on the banks of the Potomac, on land that had been ceded by Maryland and Virginia and designated as the future capital of the young Republic.

One day late in June 1791 Washington and L'Enfant walked purposefully across the fields of the new Federal District. The time had come to announce to the local landowners which sites had been selected for the principal public buildings — the Capitol, the President's House, and the headquarters of the several departments. The two men had tentatively agreed some time earlier on the sites, but now they were making a last tour of inspection before their decisions became final and were officially announced.

They were absolutely sure that they had selected the best spot for the Capitol. The wooded prominence known as Jenkins Hill was the only hill of consequence in the generally flat district; it would be a properly dominant site for the nation's two-chamber legislature.

Walking across the property of a hard-drinking Scotsman named David Burnes, Washington and L'Enfant viewed once more the spot that Washington himself had suggested for the President's House. It was, the two men still agreed, a wise choice, although they decided that day to move the actual location of the mansion slightly westward.

The house was to be erected on high ground above a picturesque though sluggish stream known as Goose Creek. Many years earlier it had been christened the Tiber by a planter named Pope who evidently had

delusions of grandeur (he called his plantation Rome). But local hunters knew that the tidal swamps around the creek were an ideal place to shoot wildfowl, and they had given the stream its less imposing name. One mile to the east was the Capitol site. Between Jenkins Hill and the place now designated for the Chief Executive's mansion, David Burnes's cornfields flourished; they would remain undisturbed until 1796, when they would be cleared to make way for Pennsylvania Avenue.

Directly to the north of the spot selected for the house — the President's Palace, as L'Enfant persisted in calling it — was a cherry orchard. One mile to the west was the small but prosperous port of Georgetown, from which Maryland and Virginia tobacco was shipped to market. Across the Potomac was another growing port, Alexandria, Virginia, which could be seen from the site of the President's House.

In every way it seemed a promising and attractive area, and Washington and L'Enfant must have been pleased and confident when they made the official announcement of their choices. They could not have known then that years of frustration and delay lay ahead; that squabbles, lack of funds, and labor problems would seriously endanger the fulfillment of their dream. Nor could they have known that L'Enfant would be fired from the project to build the new capital within the year, and that Washington would be dead by the time the President's House was ready to be occupied.

Arguments and dissension had swirled around the Federal District — soon to be called Washington by everyone but the President himself — ever since the

Washington

J. Adams

Jefferson

Madison

idea of a permanent capital was first broached. Everyone agreed that a capital was needed, but there was no concurrence on where it should be situated. Congress was then sitting in New York, where Washington lived first in a brick house on Cherry Street and later in a four-story mansion on lower Broadway. But New York was not deemed suitable for a permanent capital, nor was any other large city; it was feared that mob action might intimidate Congress in times of crisis. Philadelphia had its partisans, but it was also dismissed as a possibility — not only because of its size but also because its residents included a group of wealthy Francophiles who might have exercised an undue influence over foreign policy.

It was agreed that a virgin site, somewhere near the geographical center of the country, as it was then constituted, would be ideal. Alexander Hamilton, Washington's brilliant but autocratic Secretary of the Treasury, favored Germantown, Pennsylvania, and was supported by northern congressmen. The southerners, however, insisted that a site on the Potomac River would be more appropriate.

Like so many stalemated issues in the early days of the nation, the question was decided as part of a larger compromise. Another major problem being debated at the time was payment of the debts incurred by the various states during the Revolution. All the states had borrowed heavily to finance the war, but after victory had been attained only the southern states had begun to repay their debts. The northern states had maintained that the new national government should assume the obligations. Understandably, the South now opposed national assumption of all state debts since

southerners would be taxed as heavily as northerners to pay off what by then had become essentially northern debts.

Hamilton and Thomas Jefferson, Secretary of State and a Virginian, concocted the compromise that was eventually enacted: the South would agree to the assumption of state debts by the federal government, and the North would agree to locate the permanent capital on the Potomac.

In July 1790 Congress therefore passed the so-called Residence Bill, authorizing Washington to select a site "not exceeding ten miles square" on the Potomac. The government was to move there in 1800. Until then, a temporary capital would be established at Philadelphia.

Washington and his wife, Martha, took up residence in a comfortable house owned by Robert Morris at 190 High Street, Philadelphia. The President regarded it as "the best *single* House in the City. . . . There are good Stables . . . and a Coach House which will hold all my Carriages."

By the following January, Washington had selected the actual acreage that would comprise the Federal District and had appointed three commissioners to oversee the project. L'Enfant arrived in March. Since he had served as an engineer in the Continental Army and had later designed the seal for the Society of the Cincinnati, an organization of Revolutionary War officers, he was no stranger to Washington, who nevertheless misspelled his name as "Longfont."

The Frenchman's plan for the Federal District was clearly influenced by Versailles. He envisioned a "city of magnificent distances." Broad, tree-lined boulevards would cut diagonally across the city. There would be

many large circles, squares, and parks — the President's House, for instance, would stand on an eighty-acre site — and a rushing cascade would be created near the Capitol. It was a grandiose plan, and despite its impractical aspects it thrilled the President, who gave L'Enfant authority to turn his vision into reality.

The two men worked together closely, choosing the various sites and discussing numerous problems. But L'Enfant was a temperamental man who could not accept criticism or agree to compromise. Once, for example, when a private house was erected on a spot he deemed unsuitable, he had the house torn down, much to its owner's fury. His extravagance, insolence, and secretiveness were doing incalculable damage to the entire project, and Washington had no choice but to fire him.

L'Enfant's unfortunate departure deprived the Federal District of its chief guiding hand. Nevertheless, work continued. In June 1792 the results of the open competition for designs for the President's House were announced. The winner was James Hoban, an Irishman who had come to the United States after the Revolution and established himself as an architect. (One of his advertisements in Philadelphia read as follows: "Any gentleman who wishes to build in an elegant style, may hear of a person probably calculated for that purpose, who can execute the Joining and Carpenter's business in the modern taste.")

Hoban's design called for a simple but well-proportioned boxlike structure, three stories high. It was handsome and dignified, if not strikingly original. Its similarity to several European mansions has often been pointed out, but it was probably inspired by a plan included in a contemporary volume, James Gibbs's *A Book of Architecture*. One great virtue of the design was that it was infinitely expandable — wings could be added at both ends of the house without destroying the proportions. The most interesting feature of the interior plan was a large, oval-shaped drawing room — today's Blue Room — at the center of the building's south front.

One of the other entries in the competition had been submitted anonymously by Thomas Jefferson. More ornate than Hoban's, it was based on the work of Andrea Palladio, a sixteenth-century Italian, and called for a domed mansion with porticoes.

Washington and his commissioners chose Hoban's design not only because they thought it appropriate but also because Hoban, as a professional architect, could personally supervise the construction. He was awarded a gold medal worth five hundred dollars, a plot of land for his own use, and the job of erecting the President's House.

Hoban had guessed that the mansion could be built for about $400,000. Like all estimates concerning the Federal District, it proved to be low. Right from the beginning, money was in short supply. Virginia and Maryland, having ceded jurisdiction over the land comprising the district, had also agreed to contribute $200,000 toward construction of the public buildings. The remainder Washington had hoped to raise via a clever scheme he had convinced the local landowners to accept. Land for the public buildings would be purchased from the owners for about sixty-seven dollars an acre. The rest of the district would be divided up into lots and sold at auction, with the proceeds from the

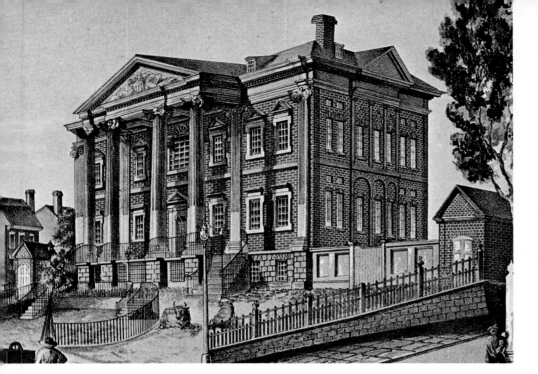

In Edward Savage's portrait of the Washingtons and their grandchildren (opposite), Martha points to a map of the Federal City, where the White House was still abuilding when the President died. The first presidential mansion, Government House in New York (left, above), was never used as such. After the capital was moved to Philadelphia in 1790, Washington lived in the Robert Morris home on High Street (left, below), where he used the mirror above, now hanging in the White House.

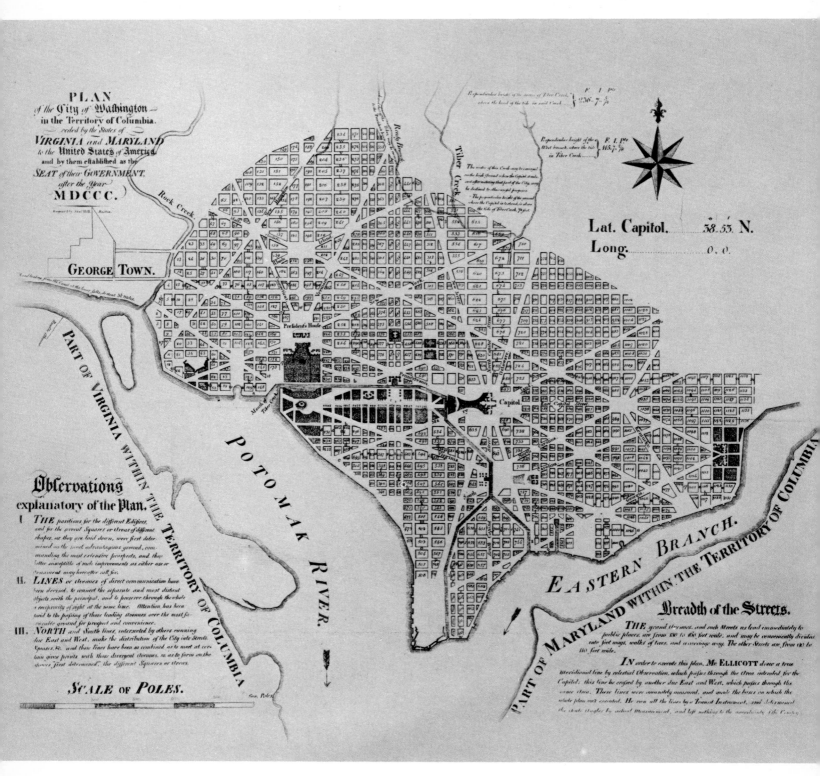

sale of every other lot going to the government to finance construction of the government buildings. The land for streets would be provided free by the new proprietors — a seemingly minor request agreed to readily by the landowners, who later protested when they saw how much land would be required for L'Enfant's broad avenues.

It was a good plan, but in actuality it proved disappointing. Few people shared Washington's conviction that the district had a glorious future, and the prices brought by the auctioned land were surprisingly low. It therefore became necessary to badger Congress for more funds, and to finance and refinance, beg and borrow, with monotonous regularity.

Cutbacks of all kinds were instituted to save money. Hoban agreed, for example, to eliminate the third floor of the President's House as an economy move. It was also decided not to build the porticoes Hoban had envisioned. Lack of strong supervision slowed the whole Federal District project, as did the periodic fighting among the commissioners, the architects, and the laborers. Pressure to abandon the whole scheme increased; Pennsylvania went so far as to begin constructing permanent buildings for the federal government in Philadelphia, in the hope that the district on the Potomac would be forsaken.

The fact that work on the Federal District continued year after year despite all obstacles was due chiefly to President Washington's unwavering support and his confidence that his dream would be realized. When he left office early in 1797, he stopped at the site of the President's House during his journey from Philadelphia to Mount Vernon. But he did not live to see the

The original plan for the city of Washington, shown in the 1800 map opposite, called for a series of parks, squares, and broad, radiating avenues, with Pennsylvania Avenue connecting the Capitol and the President's House. Above, James Hoban's prize-winning design for the White House features Georgian-style balustrades, a hipped roof, and alternating window arches. Hoban's floor plan (below) included an oval drawing room (today's Blue Room) and a colonnaded south portico that was not built. The staircase at right in the drawing was removed during the renovation of 1902 in order to enlarge the State Dining Room (E).

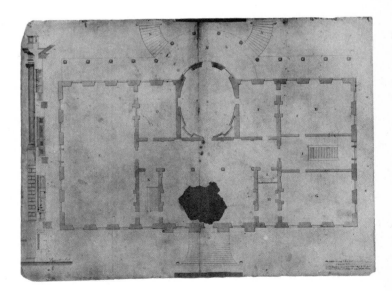

Georgetown and the sparsely settled Federal City are shown in the engraving at right, as they appeared to an artist in 1801. Despite the pastoral beauty of the surroundings, congressmen protested that they were "utterly secluded from society"—and Abigail Adams, the first First Lady to live in the White House, complained that Georgetown was "a quagmire after every rain." Her silhouette is shown at left, above the words of John Adams — later inscribed on the mantel in the State Dining Room by F.D.R.

completed building. He died in 1799, the year the sandstone walls were finally finished and roofed over.

The interior of the mansion was, of course, far from finished, as John Adams, the second President, noted with dismay when he visited the district in May 1800. Nevertheless, the government was scheduled to move to Washington that year and move it did — with all 130 federal employees.

For Adams the move was merely one more unpleasant event in a Presidency that had given him little pleasure. Opposed at every turn by the followers of his Vice President, Thomas Jefferson, the President was also at loggerheads with members of his own Federalist party, particularly Alexander Hamilton. An undeclared naval war with France and bitterness at home over the unpopular Alien and Sedition laws had made his administration a difficult one. And yet John Adams, who seemed so pompous and cantankerous to those who were not aware of the deep convictions and complete integrity beneath the frosty veneer, still hoped for a second term. Cheering crowds along his route from Philadelphia to the Federal District buoyed his hopes.

The President's spirits undoubtedly fell when he reached the Executive Mansion on November 1, 1800, saw the workmen's shacks and the rubble on the grounds around it, and then discovered that some of the walls in the cold, damp house were still unplastered and that the main central staircase had not yet been erected.

That first night Adams wrote to his wife, Abigail: "I pray Heaven to bestow the best of Blessings on this House and all that shall hereafter inhabit it. May none but honest and wise Men ever rule under this roof."

Many years later another President, Franklin Delano Roosevelt, would have those words carved on the mantel of the State Dining Room.

It is to Abigail, John Adams's perceptive and loyal wife, that we owe the most accurate account of those first days in the President's House. Arriving in the Federal District two weeks after her husband, she was appalled by what she found:

Not one room or chamber is finished of the whole. It is habitable by fires in every part, thirteen of which we are obliged to keep daily, or sleep in wet and damp places. To assist us in this great castle, and render less attendance necessary, bells are wholly wanting . . . and promises are all you can obtain. This is so great an inconvenience that I know not what to do!

Congress had appropriated $25,000 to furnish the mansion, but the results of such an expenditure were not evident to Abigail. There were, she bemoaned, no adequate lamps or proper mirrors. She could not get sufficient firewood. And there was no yard in which she could dry her laundry. The huge East Room, unfinished and unplastered, was pressed into unlikely service by the First Lady, who hung her wash to dry there — thus giving rise to one of the building's most cherished legends.

Abigail was far too intelligent a woman to allow the inconveniences of the moment to obscure the prospects for the future. "But this House is built for ages to come," she wrote a relative, adding that "The establishment necessary is a task which cannot be born by the present sallery." She was thus the first — but hardly the last — White House occupant to decry the differential between the President's income and the

expenses of running the Executive Mansion. It would require, she estimated, thirty servants to staff the house properly.

Abigail was soon writing in a slightly more optimistic frame of mind:

Six chambers are made comfortable; two are occupied by the President and Mr. Shaw; two lower rooms, one for a common parlour, and one for a levee-room. Up stairs there is the oval room, which is designed for the drawingroom, and has the crimson furniture in it. It is a very handsome room now; but, when completed, it will be beautiful.

The location of the mansion, she felt, left little to desire. It was, she wrote, "in a beautiful situation in front of which is the Potomac with a view of Alexandria. The country round is romantic but a wild wilderness at present." (There were only about forty real houses in the central area of the district at the time; it was because of the housing shortage that the workmen had to live in shacks on the mansion's grounds.)

For Georgetown, Abigail had no kind words. She described it as "the very dirtyest Hole I ever saw for a place of any trade. . . . It is only one mile from me, but a quagmire after every rain."

Quagmire or not, Georgetown had its share of social-minded ladies who implored the First Lady to hold court at the new mansion. So, as they had done in Philadelphia, the Adamses held weekly levees for foreign ministers, congressmen, and the ladies of Georgetown. Adams, often dressed in black velvet breeches with silver buckles at his knees, stood stiffly behind his wife on a low dais in the Oval Room, greeting guests with a regal bow and never relaxing for a moment.

The ladies of Georgetown were happy, but not for long. Adams lived in the President's House for only four months; his wish for a second term was not granted. He was supplanted in March 1801 by Thomas Jefferson.

In contrast to the courtlike atmosphere created by the Adamses, Jefferson brought to the mansion a wonderful combination of informality and elegance. He immediately abolished the formal levees, except on New Year's Day and the Fourth of July, and instead of bowing to his guests he shook their hands. The Federalists and visiting foreigners were shocked, but to Jefferson it seemed proper behavior for the leader of a democracy.

In place of formal receptions, Jefferson gave small dinner parties, usually for fourteen people or less. Mrs. Margaret Bayard Smith, a friend of Jefferson, defended his innovations:

If in his manner he was simple, affable and unceremonious, it was not because he was ignorant of, but because he despised the conventional and artificial usages of courts and fashionable life. . . . At his usual dinner parties . . . his guests were generally selected in reference to their tastes, habits and suitability in all respects, which attention had a wonderful effect in making his parties more agreeable, than dinner parties usually are. . . . At Mr. Jefferson's table the conversation was general; every guest was entertained and interested in whatever topic was discussed. To each an opportunity was offered for the exercise of his colloquial powers and the stream of conversation thus enriched by such various contributions flowed on full, free and animated; of course he took the lead and gave the tone with *tact* so true and discriminating that he

The design at left, entered anonymously in the competition for the President's House, was actually the work of Thomas Jefferson, and in style it somewhat resembles Monticello, the Virginia home he designed for himself. Jefferson, shown at right in a 1791 portrait by Charles Willson Peale, seems to have preferred the scale of his own designs, for he found the White House "big enough for two emperors, one pope and the grand lama."

seldom missed his aim, which was to draw forth the talents and information of each and all of his guests and to place every one in an advantageous light and by being pleased with themselves . . . please others.

To avoid seating by rank, Jefferson had a round table installed in his dining room — that way no one was seated below the salt. He also paid little attention to the order in which guests entered the dining room, an omission which infuriated the British ambassador who felt that his wife should have been the first lady taken in to dinner. It was that same ambassador, Anthony Merry, who was outraged when he was taken to the presidential mansion to meet Jefferson for the first time and found the President "not merely in undress, but actually standing in slippers down at the heels, and both pantaloons, coat and underclothes, indicative of utter slovenliness and indifference to appearances, and in a state of negligence actually studied. . . ."

Unlike Merry, most guests at the President's House thought themselves lucky to have been invited. The company was exhilarating and the food and wine superb. Jefferson's French steward, Lamar, went to the Georgetown market each morning, and the President often accompanied him. They sometimes spent as much as fifty dollars there in a single expedition. In his first year as President, Jefferson spent $6,500 on food and provisions alone, and additional thousands on wine. It rapidly became apparent to him, as it had to Abigail Adams, that the President's annual salary — $25,000 at the time — would not cover all the expenses incurred in office.

Dinner at the President's House was usually served at four in the afternoon, in a small room on the south front of the mansion that is now known as the Green Room. A typical meal was described by Manasseh Cutler, a clergyman who dined with Jefferson in 1802. The menu included rice soup, round of beef, ham, turkey, mutton, veal cutlets, and "a pie called maca-roni." Dessert was also notable: "Ice cream very good, crust wholly dried, crumbled into thin flakes; a dish somewhat like a pudding — inside white as milk or curd, very porous and light, covered with cream sauce — very fine. Many other jim cracks, a great variety of fruit, plenty of wine, and good." Another novelty served by Jefferson's French chef was "pannequaiques," which the President enjoyed so much that he wrote to one of his daughters about it.

Because he was a widower — Martha Jefferson had died in 1782, leaving him with three small daughters to raise — the third President asked the vivacious wife of James Madison, his Secretary of State, to serve as his hostess. Dolley Madison filled the role superbly. She also guided his married daughters around Washington whenever they came to spend time with their father. During Jefferson's Presidency, one of his grandsons was born in the mansion, the first White House baby.

Many decades later, President John F. Kennedy spoke of Thomas Jefferson to a group of Nobel Prize winners who had been invited to dine with him. The Nobel laureates were, Kennedy told them, "the most extraordinary collection of talent . . . that has ever been gathered at the White House — with the possible exception of when Thomas Jefferson dined alone."

Kennedy referred, of course, to the astonishing breadth of Jefferson's abilities and interests, signs of which were greatly in evidence at the Executive Man-

These drawings, by Benjamin Henry Latrobe (far right), Jefferson's surveyor of public buildings, show Latrobe's additions to the White House. The low-lying terrace pavilions (center) were completed toward the end of Jefferson's term in office and are similar to pavilions the President himself designed for Monticello and the University of Virginia. The rectangular North Portico and the rounded South Portico (near right) were completed by 1829.

sion during his Presidency. Jefferson was a philosopher, a musician, a lawyer, a farmer, a linguist, a botanist, a writer, a scientist, a naturalist. He was interested in literally everything. Knowing of his fondness for the natural sciences, Lewis and Clark sent him a collection of bones during their epic cross-continental expedition of 1804–6; the bones were installed in a room in the President's House, where Jefferson spent hours studying them. The two explorers also sent him grizzly bears, which for a time were kept in a cage on the grounds of the mansion. (Meriwether Lewis, incidentally, had served as Jefferson's private secretary prior to his western journey. He had lived in the still-unplastered East Room, where temporary partitions had been erected to make quarters for him.)

Jefferson's own inventions were used throughout the house. For instance, in the dining room he installed various dumbwaiters and other devices so that guests might serve themselves and not be interrupted by servants during important diplomatic or political discussions.

Another passionate interest of the President was architecture, and he oversaw the completion and improvement of the mansion with pleasure. Working with the American architect Benjamin H. Latrobe, he had low terraces built onto both ends of the house, along with a number of necessary small buildings such as stables and storehouses. He played an active role in landscaping the grounds around the house, seeing to it that the workmen's shacks were removed at last and that elms and magnolias were planted. A wall was built around the grounds to provide some privacy.

The interior of the house was furnished with exqui-

site French pieces, many of which Jefferson had purchased while he was minister to France after the Revolution. It was during Jefferson's Presidency that Gilbert Stuart's famous portrait of Washington was hung in the Oval Room. During Adams's stay in the mansion, that beautiful chamber had served as a reception room for visitors entering from the south side. Jefferson closed off the south entrance, however, and had his guests come in from the north instead.

Toward the end of Jefferson's second four-year term, Latrobe was shocked to discover that although the East Room had never been completed, it was already in a state of disrepair. The roof, he warned, might fall in at any moment. Indeed, the entire mansion needed repairs. "It is a duty which I owe to myself and the public, not to conceal that the timbers of the President's House are in a very considerable decay," he wrote in 1809.

That same year Jefferson returned to private life. His Presidency had had its triumphs, chief among them the Louisiana Purchase, which vastly expanded the nation's territory. But he had been plagued by ever-increasing foreign problems; relations with England and France had grown dangerously unfriendly. That, however, was now a problem for his successor, James Madison. It was with great pleasure that Jefferson retired to Monticello — pleasure at having served his country long and well, pleasure at being able to return to his beloved home, pleasure at seeing his protégé and close friend succeed him as President.

Now Dolley Madison was First Lady in her own right. Not until Jacqueline Kennedy's day a century and a half later would an equally glamorous figure

dominate the social scene in Washington.

Dolley was forty-one when her husband became President; he was fifty-eight. They had been married happily since 1794, shortly after the widowed Dolley Payne Todd was introduced by Aaron Burr to the young Virginia congressman.

Few wives have helped their husbands' careers more than Dolley did. Although she was not a beautiful woman, she combined, as Margaret Bayard Smith wrote, "all the elegance and polish of fashion" with "the unadulterated simplicity, frankness, warmth, and friendliness of her native character." As First Lady she blossomed. Her elegant dinners and weekly receptions provided a gay and relaxed atmosphere in which business was profitably mixed with pleasure. Congressmen and foreign diplomats, softened and mellowed by good food and the ministrations of the charming Dolley, were far more willing to compromise or listen to other opinions than they would have been under less pleasant conditions.

Dressed elegantly in expensive gowns of the latest fashion and wearing the elaborate turbans that became her trademark, Dolley had a compliment or an interesting remark for everyone. She could put almost anyone at ease — if not by a *bon mot* of her own concoction, then by reading an interesting passage from a popular romance or by offering a pinch of snuff from the ornate snuffbox she always carried with her. Men adored her, and so — surprisingly — did most of their wives. Dolley made a point of returning all calls made upon her; on some days she herself made as many as fifteen courtesy calls.

When the Madisons moved into the President's House, Congress appropriated $12,000 for repairs and improvements and $14,000 for items needed by the household. Latrobe directed the renovations and expenditures. At Dolley's urging, a piano was purchased — at a cost of $458. She also obtained a service of blue Lowestoft china for her state dinners and ordered a new carriage that cost $1,500. Latrobe himself designed elegant furniture in Greek Revival style for the Oval Room, which was also adorned with yellow damask curtains.

By this time the term "White House" was in general use. For many years historians believed that the name was not used until after the mansion had been burned by the British and its blackened walls repainted. Research has since indicated that the building was known as the White House as early as 1809. The name did not become official, however, until Theodore Roosevelt's administration at the beginning of the twentieth century.

But whether it was known as the White House, the Executive Mansion, or the President's House, it was a magnet for visitors to Washington who had heard of Dolley Madison's constant round of levees, lawn parties, dances, and receptions of all kinds. Washington Irving, for instance, could not resist attending one of the Wednesday evening levees when he visited the capital. Like everyone else, he was charmed by the First Lady. "Mrs. Madison is a fine, portly, buxom dame who has a smile and a pleasant word for everybody," he wrote. Irving was not, however, impressed by the President, whom he described as "a withered little apple-John."

Certainly Madison, who at five-foot-six and barely one hundred pounds is the smallest President in the

THE FALL of WASHINGTON ... or Maddy in Full Flight.

Reveling in their country's victory, British cartoonists portrayed the burning of Washington in August 1814. At right, a British officer conducts the attack from the heights above the city, while the White House (K) goes up in flames. At left, pursued by the gibes of both Englishmen and Americans, President Madison and a friend flee the city with heaps of papers, including plans for the conquest of Canada and the bill of fare for an abruptly terminated Cabinet supper.

nation's history, was not an impressive figure physically. He could, however, be as charming and as witty as his wife when his mind was clear of worry.

Unfortunately, he was more often than not preoccupied with the cares of his office, especially with foreign affairs. Conflict with France and England grew as both countries, at war with each other, harassed American shipping. The British went so far as to search American vessels and remove any sailors they regarded as British citizens. Indian troubles in the West were also thought to have been instigated by the British.

A group of young western congressmen, known as the War Hawks, demanded that the United States defend its honor by declaring war. Some of them hoped that war with England would result in the acquisition of Canada by the United States. New England, on the other hand, found its shipping profitable despite the harassment and was solidly against war.

By 1812, an economic depression had struck England; it would probably have led to an easing of British provocation of the United States. In fact, the French under Napoleon posed a greater threat to the security of the young nation than did the British. But Madison was unable to withstand the pressures at home; on June 1, 1812, he asked Congress to declare war on England.

It was a war that accomplished little, if anything. Some dramatic American victories at sea had little effect, and American attempts to invade Canada were unsuccessful. Andrew Jackson's victory at New Orleans on January 8, 1815, was impressive, but ironically it occurred two weeks after the Treaty of Ghent, ending the war, had been signed in Europe. The treaty did not

change the status quo, nor did it contain assurances that America's grievances would be redressed.

The most dramatic event of the fruitless war was, of course, the burning of Washington.

In August 1814 four thousand British troops aboard a fleet commanded by Vice Admiral Sir Alexander Cochrane sailed into Chesapeake Bay and up the Patuxent River, where they disembarked. At the White House, Dolley Madison hurriedly packed important documents, silver plate, the velvet curtains, and a collection of small valuables as she waited for news from her husband, who had gone to Bladensburg, Maryland, seven miles northeast of the capital, to watch American troops engage the British. Before leaving her, Dolley wrote on August 23, the President had:

enquired anxiously whether I had courage, or firmness to remain in the President's house until his return, on the morrow, or succeeding day. . . . I have since recd two despatches from him written with a pencil . . . he desires I should be ready at a moment's warning to enter my carriage and leave the city. . . . I am determined not to go myself until I see Mr. Madison safe, and he can accompany me. . . .

The following day at Bladensburg an American force twice as large as the British contingent turned tail and fled after barely a shot had been fired. From the roof of the White House, Dolley saw the retreating troops through her spyglass. That afternoon she wrote to her sister: "We have had a battle, or skirmish near Bladensburg, and I am still here within sound of the cannon! . . . Two messengers, covered with dust, come to bid me fly; but I wait for him. . . ."

Eventually, Dolley acquiesced to pleas that she leave

Its interior gutted by flames, the White House was left a blackened shell after the British attack on the capital. (The twisted object rising from the roof in the aquatint at right is probably a lightning rod, bent by the heat of the fire.) Dolley Madison, shown at left in a painting by Gilbert Stuart on display in the Red Room, fled the scene only after rescuing Stuart's portrait of Washington (left, below). The only White House object dating from the days of the mansion's first occupancy in 1800, the Washington portrait traditionally hangs in the East Room, paired with a later likeness of Martha Washington.

without her husband. Just before departing, she arranged for the Gilbert Stuart portrait of George Washington to be removed:

> Our kind friend, Mr Carrol, has come to hasten my departure, and is in a very bad humor with me because I insist on waiting until the large picture of Gen. Washington is secured, and it requires to be unscrewed from the wall. This process was found too tedious for these perilous moments; I have ordered the frame to be broken and the canvas taken out; it is done, — and the precious portrait placed in the hands of two gentlemen of New York, for safe keeping.

Dolley fled to safety and was soon reunited with her husband. Meanwhile, the British troops, commanded by Major General Robert Ross and Rear Admiral Sir George Cockburn, entered the capital and methodically set it aflame. That evening the fires burned so brightly that observers said it looked like daytime. The Capitol and the other public buildings were burning, and so was the White House.

Before setting fire to the Executive Mansion, Admiral Cockburn and his men had eaten food that had been left on a table and had drunk vulgar toasts to "Jemmy's health" with the President's own wine. As souvenirs, Cockburn helped himself to one of Madison's hats and one of Dolley's cushions. His men then systematically piled tables and chairs in the drawing room and started a bonfire that soon engulfed the building. Only a heavy storm later that night prevented the total demolition of the President's House. As it was, the inside was gutted and the roof destroyed; only the blackened walls remained standing.

The British marched cockily on to Baltimore but

found to their surprise that the burning of the capital — instead of demoralizing their enemy — had stiffened the resolve of the American soldiers. Unable to capture the city, the British embarked for Jamaica; it was from there that they headed for New Orleans, where Jackson defeated them soundly the following January.

William Wirt, an American lawyer, visited the White House soon after the Madisons returned to the city:

I went to look at the ruins of the President's House. The rooms which you saw so richly furnished, exhibited nothing but unroofed, naked walls, cracked, defaced, and blackened with fire. I cannot tell you what I felt as I walked among them. . . . I called on the President. He looks miserably shattered and woebegone. In short, he looks heartbroken.

Despair did not long reign in the capital, however. Washington somehow convinced itself that the peace treaty was an American triumph, and Jackson's thrilling victory at New Orleans restored the nation's self-respect. Dolley soon began entertaining as lavishly and as frequently as ever — not at the White House, of course, but a short distance away at the Madisons' new residence, the Octagon House, which had been the home of the French ambassador.

Suggestions that Washington be abandoned and the capital moved elsewhere were rejected, and the laborious task of rebuilding was begun. It fell to James Hoban, the original architect, to direct the restoration of the White House.

At the end of his second term, in March 1817, James and Dolley Madison returned to their Virginia plantation, where they were plagued by ever-increasing debts. When the former President died in 1836, his widow returned to Washington and, despite her financial problems, resumed her active role in the capital's social life. Dolley had to mortgage her house on Lafayette Square, and her neighbor Daniel Webster often sent baskets of food around to her kitchen without her knowledge. But successive occupants of the White House continued to ask her advice on social matters, and no occasion seemed official without her presence.

Her last appearance at the White House was in 1848, at a ball given by President Polk. Radiant in a white satin gown with a fringed turban of the same material, she took the President's arm and made her way graciously through the crowded rooms. Later that year she attended the cornerstone ceremonies for the Washington Monument. It was her last public appearance. Born seven years before the outbreak of the Revolution, Dolley Madison died at the age of eighty-one, twelve years before the start of the Civil War.

In the White House today there are only a few items that belonged to the Madisons. Among them are pieces from Dolley's French porcelain dinner service and Gilbert Stuart's lovely portrait of her, which hangs now, as it did during the Madison Presidency, in the Red Room. Displayed in the second-floor dining room is Madison's walnut medicine chest, returned to the Executive Mansion in 1939 by the Canadian descendant of a British soldier who had taken it as a souvenir when the mansion was set aflame in 1814.

II
Elegance and Egalitarianism

The charming weather of yesterday," commented the *National Intelligencer* on January 2, 1818, "contributed to enliven the reciprocal salutations of kindness and good wishes which are customary at every return of New Year's Day. The President's House, for the first time since its reaerification, was thrown open for the general reception of visitors. It was thronged from 12 to 3 o'clock. . . . It was gratifying once more to be able to salute the President of the United States with the compliments of the season in his appropriate residence."

James Monroe had succeeded Madison as President in March 1817, but not until that fall had the rebuilt White House been ready to receive the new First Family, and not until New Year's Day did the Monroes open the mansion for a public reception.

Naturally, all Washington flocked to see the redecorated palace, the exterior of which gleamed with a fresh coat of white paint. The mansion was not yet fully furnished, but the New Year's Day guests must have been impressed and pleased by what they saw.

The Monroes had spent many years abroad in the diplomatic service, and they had become unabashed admirers of French furnishings. A total sum of $50,000 had been allocated by Congress to furnish the White House, and most of that money was spent in France. Several years later, in 1822, Congress passed a law requiring that furniture for the White House be bought in the United States whenever possible, but the rule was never enforced. And by that time the mansion was well stocked with superb French pieces.

To begin with, the Monroes had generously sold to the government their own furniture, purchased during their stay in France. Each item was carefully appraised before it was installed in the White House (a mustard pot, for example, was valued at 9.56\frac{1}{4}$), and the President was paid $9,071.22$\frac{1}{2}$ for the entire collection.

To augment that initial sale, the Monroes ordered innumerable items from France, using Russell and LaFarge, an American firm with an office in Bordeaux, as agents. Russell and LaFarge procured whatever the Monroes requested, gave them advice (mahogany furniture was not deemed suitable for a gentleman's drawing room, they wrote, but gilded wood was proper), and usually spent more money on purchases than had originally been budgeted. On one occasion, for instance, they wrote to the President:

> The furniture for the large Oval Room, is much higher than the prices limited. It must be ascribed to the gilt-wood and crimson silk trimmings, fringes, etc., which is 50 per cent dearer than other colors. . . . The christal and gilt bronze lustre is of superior workmanship . . . and if it was to be made again would cost 5,000 francs.

The artisans of France may have raised their prices when the words "President's Palace" were mentioned, but the result was a White House of great elegance.

The Oval Room was especially attractive when the Monroes had completed furnishing it. On the floor was an Aubusson rug of green velvet, with the arms of the United States incorporated into the pattern. The sofas were covered in pinkish-red silk, as were the chairs and stools. From archways decorated with carved eagles hung red taffeta draperies. And all around the room, and indeed all through the mansion, were exquisite clocks, candelabra, vases, and other pieces of bronze-doré and porcelain, imported from France.

Monroe

J. Q. Adams

Jackson

Van Buren

Most fabulous of all was an ornate thirteen-foot-long centerpiece of carved bronze, used in the State Dining Room. Built in seven main sections, it featured numerous figurines, candle holders, vases, and pedestals, many of which — being detachable — were items of beauty and utility in their own right.

Obviously, the James Monroes believed in living elegantly and in impressing White House visitors. Monroe was, after all, a veteran of the Revolution — he had been wounded at Trenton — and having fought to create a new nation, he understandably wished foreign guests to be aware of the young country's prosperity and stability. As a diplomat in Europe he had seen the pomp and ceremony of Old World governments, and he deemed it important that the President of the United States live in surroundings of luxury.

But after the egalitarian Jefferson and the spontaneously charming Dolley Madison, the Monroes seemed to Washington's residents to be far too formal and pompous. Right from the beginning of her husband's Presidency, Elizabeth Monroe, an aristocratic New Yorker, was accused of snobbishness. Unlike Dolley Madison, who returned all calls, Elizabeth announced that she would return none, nor would she receive casual visitors at the White House. Both decisions, in retrospect, seem practical, but at the time they created a furor. Elizabeth Monroe also made the mistake of greeting guests from a raised platform, which smacked of monarchy to the oversensitive.

To make matters worse, the Monroes' oldest daughter, Eliza Hay, really was a snob ("An obstinate firebrand," Secretary of State John Quincy Adams called her). Eliza had been educated in Paris and had numbered princesses among her classmates; evidently she regarded herself as something of a princess too. She offended much of official Washington with her airs and tactlessness. When, for instance, the other Monroe daughter, Maria Hester, was married in the White House in 1820, Eliza decided that only the family and close friends would be invited to what she designated a "New York style" wedding. When the Russian minister asked her what the foreign diplomats could do to mark the marriage, Eliza told him rudely to ignore it. (Maria Hester, by the way, was the first President's daughter to be married in the White House. The wedding ceremony took place in the Oval Room, and she and her groom, Samuel Gouverneur, repeated their vows while standing on the letters U. S. in the Aubusson carpet.)

For a while, the ladies of the capital were so upset by the Monroes' aloofness and Eliza's blunders that they boycotted the White House, refusing to attend the weekly "drawing-rooms" there. After one such affair Mrs. William Seaton, the wife of a newspaper editor, noted that "the drawing-room of the President was opened last night to a beggarly row of empty chairs. Only five females attended, three of whom were foreigners."

Even the more intimate dinner parties at the White House suffered from rigid formality. A congressman described one dinner in 1818: At 5:30 he was ushered into the East Room. Mrs. Monroe sat at one end of the room with several ladies. Sitting in a chair at the center of the room was the President, his hair powdered as was his custom. The male guests sat solemnly against a wall. New arrivals shook hands with the host and hostess and then sat down quietly against the wall. "Not

The sumptuous decor of the State Dining Room (left) is enhanced by a splendid collection of French bronze-doré, bought for the restored White House in 1817 by President Monroe, whose taste for formality and elegance irked republican spirits. The plateau at the center of the near table and the fruit basket at right are among the most treasured historic pieces in the White House collection, and are often used to decorate the tables at state dinners.

a whisper broke upon the ear to interrupt the silence of the place," the congressman reported, "and everyone looked as if the next moment would be his last." When Monroe finally decided to address a remark to someone, he was interrupted in mid-sentence as more guests were ushered toward him. Half an hour later, dinner was announced. Although the food was good and the table "richly-furnished," it could scarcely be counted a scintillating evening.

As the administration progressed, Washington got used to the Monroes, and perhaps the Monroes loosened up a bit themselves, becoming more comfortable in their roles as President and First Lady. Their dinners retained what James Fenimore Cooper had called "rather a cold than a formal air," but their receptions were again well attended — which must have caused the Monroes some mixed feelings if the following contemporary account of a Monroe open house was accurate:

The secretaries, senators, foreign ministers, consuls, auditors, accountants, officers of the army and navy of every grade, farmers, merchants, parsons, priests, lawyers, judges, auctioneers, and nothing-arians — all with their wives and some with their gawky offspring, crowd to the President's House every Wednesday evening; some in shoes, most in boots and many in spurs; some snuffing, others chewing, and many longing for their cigars and whiskey-punch left at home; some with powdered heads, others frizzled and oiled, whose heads a comb has never touched, and which are half-hid by dirty collars as stiff as pasteboard.

Monroe may have had his social troubles, but in other respects his Presidency was quite successful. He won all but one electoral vote in the election of 1820 — the sole dissenter held that the honor of unanimous election to the Presidency should belong only to George Washington — and his administration was known as "The Era of Good Feelings." During his Presidency, Florida was obtained from Spain, the Missouri Compromise solved temporarily the problem of the expansion of slavery, and the Monroe Doctrine — drafted by John Quincy Adams — confidently warned foreign powers that the Western Hemisphere was off limits to them.

Ironically, Monroe's Presidency ended with a contretemps over the 1817–18 expenditures for White House furnishings. The Commissioner of Public Buildings, who had handled the funds appropriated by Congress for the mansion, had died without officially accounting for $20,000 of the total sum. When an insolent congressman summoned Monroe to Capitol Hill to testify on the matter, the President dismissed the legislator as "a scoundrel" and promptly bought back the furniture he had sold the government in 1817. He paid $9,071.22½, the same sum he had received eight years earlier.

Monroe's successor, John Quincy Adams, son of the second President, also had trouble over furnishings for the White House. He was allotted $14,000 for refurbishment, but when he bought a billiard table such a cry was raised by his enemies that he paid for it himself.

That was but one unpleasant incident in a Presidency as ill-starred as that of Adams's father. John Quincy had actually finished second to Andrew Jackson in the electoral vote of December 1824. But no one had won a majority in the four-way race, and the House

of Representatives subsequently elected Adams President. The support of Henry Clay, one of the other candidates, had been the deciding factor in Adams's election, and when Adams later made Clay Secretary of State, charges of a "corrupt bargain" proliferated.

Adams's tenure in the White House proved to be merely a sterile four-year interlude before Jackson, the popular hero of the battle of New Orleans, was swept into office. Although he was a man of vision and great intelligence, Adams was not a leader of men. He lacked tact and the ability to compromise, and he seems to have been somewhat paranoiac, seeing plots against him in every minor incident.

Life in the White House under Adams, a New Englander, contrasted sharply with the regimes of his three Virginia-born predecessors. Adams rose each day between four and six, and whenever possible he took an early swim in the Potomac. A story about a newspaper-woman sitting on the President's clothes on the river-bank and refusing to let him emerge from the water until he had granted her an exclusive interview seems to be apocryphal. It is true, however, that Adams was almost drowned when a boat he was sailing in was overturned by a sudden gale. Since he and his friends had been about to go for a swim, they had divested themselves of most of their clothing before the accident. When they finally struggled to shore, the President had to wait shivering on the bank until clothes were brought for him.

After his daily swim, the President would return to the White House, read from the Bible for a while, have breakfast, and then go to his office for a long day of work and meeting visitors. Conspicuous among his callers were office seekers, but Adams did not believe in dismissing satisfactory federal employees merely to replace them with his own supporters — a high-minded but politically naïve approach. Late in the afternoon, Adams went for a walk or a horseback ride, returning to the mansion for dinner at 5:30. He then went back to work, unless he had to act as host at one of his wife's weekly receptions, a task he did not relish. The President's wife, Louisa, was a gracious hostess, but Adams himself found making small talk difficult. Only if the conversation centered on one of his favorite subjects, such as astronomy, did he really enjoy himself. Usually, the President was asleep by eleven.

One of Adams's great joys was horticulture, and he loved to supervise the planting of trees and shrubs at the White House. The land around the mansion was filled and graded during his administration and according to Ben Perley Poore, whose reminiscences of sixty years of life in Washington were published in 1886, John Quincy Adams "had planted in the grounds of the White House the acorns of the cork-oak, black walnuts, peach, plum, and cherry stones, apple and pear seeds, and he watched their germination and growth with great interest."

Like his father before him, Adams was so resentful of his failure to win reelection that he refused to attend the inauguration of his successor. Many other members of the eastern establishment also stayed away. But the common people came in great numbers, pouring into Washington to see "Old Hickory" sworn in. All available beds were soon spoken for, and the mob slept on billiard tables, floors, or any other flat surface they could find. Andrew Jackson, a product of the western

ANDREW JACKSON'S

Inaugural Address,

On being sworn into Office, as President of the United States, March 4th, 1829.

The boisterous reception that followed Andrew Jackson's inauguration in 1829 is satirized in the caricature (far left) titled "The President's Levee, or all Creation going to the White House." At near left is a detail from a wood engraving, printed on silk, of Old Hickory's first inaugural address.
  Overleaf:
Washington in 1833 was dominated by the domed Capitol and the White House (left of center). To the right, on the Anacostia River, is the Navy yard.

frontier and a self-made man in every sense, had been elected by these people, many of whom were newly enfranchised because of the elimination of property requirements for voters in many states. "I have never seen such a crowd before," said Daniel Webster. "Persons have come five hundred miles to see General Jackson, and they really seem to think that the country has been rescued from some dreadful danger."

The "people's President" was sixty-one at the time of his inauguration. His hair was white, but he stood tall and erect, despite the personal sorrow that made the event more an ordeal than a moment of triumph for him. Jackson was overwhelmed with grief, for his beloved wife, Rachel, had died three months earlier.

Jackson was embittered as well as mournful, for he believed that his wife's death had been hastened by calumny leveled against her during the campaign. Rachel Jackson had been unhappily married to someone else in her youth, but she and Jackson had been led to believe that her first husband had obtained a divorce. Jackson married her in 1791, but was appalled to learn two years later that her husband had deceived them in the matter of the divorce, which did not actually become final until 1793. Jackson and Rachel went through the ordeal of a second marriage ceremony, but cruel gossips never let the story die. His political enemies branded Rachel an adulteress, and Jackson fought several duels over real or imagined slights to her honor. One slanderous conversation, accidentally overheard by Rachel during a shopping expedition, was thought to have precipitated the final breakdown in her already frail health.

The President-elect's personal tragedy was forgotten, however, by the boisterous crowds that thronged the Capitol on March 4, 1829 — inauguration day. To avoid being crushed by the mob, Jackson climbed over a wall and entered the Capitol from the basement. His admirers cheered as he appeared on the portico, and they cheered again after he had been sworn in by Chief Justice John Marshall. The inaugural address was uninspiring, but the crowd's enthusiasm was undampened. And as soon as the ceremony was over, the mob rushed down the still-unpaved Pennsylvania Avenue to the White House, where refreshments had been laid out.

Supreme Court Justice Joseph Story reported that the White House reception was attended by:

. . . immense crowds of all sorts of people, from the highest and the most polished, down to the most vulgar and gross in the nation. I never saw such a mixture. The reign of KING MOB seemed triumphant. I was glad to escape from the scene as soon as possible.

Story's reaction was understandable. The crowd rushed into the East Room, demolishing the refreshments, breaking dishes, ruining the furniture. Women fainted in the crush, and fights broke out. It was "a regular Saturnalia," a guest wrote to New York Governor Martin Van Buren, who had the good fortune to be elsewhere.

A particularly vivid account of the riotous reception was left by one observer:

Orange punch by barrels full was made, but as the waiters opened the door to bring it out, a rush would be made, the glasses broken, the pails of liquor upset, and the most painful confusion prevailed. To such a painful degree was this carried, that wine and ice-

A cartoonist, imagining a popular dancer prancing before Jackson and his Cabinet (right), suggested that the lady might be encouraged to disrupt the President's second term much as Peggy Eaton had disrupted the first. The picture is often used to illustrate the special Cabinet meeting that was called to discuss the Eaton affair — but Mrs. Eaton did not attend that meeting. The miniature portrait reproduced at left was one of Jackson's favorites.

creams could not be brought out to the ladies, and tubs of punch were taken from the lower story into the garden, to lead off the crowd from the rooms. On such an occasion it was certainly difficult to keep anything like order, but it was mortifying to see men, with boots heavy with mud, standing on the damask satin covered chairs, from their eagerness to get a sight of the President.

Fearful for his safety, a group of men formed a chain to keep the crowds away from Jackson and led him to a back door, through which he escaped.

If some Washingtonians were afraid that the inaugural melee had set the tone for the new administration's entertainments, their fears were soon allayed. Jackson was indeed a son of the frontier, and he was certainly determined to use the power of the Presidency to defend the rights and liberties of the common man, but he was also an affluent Southern planter who had grown accustomed to the finer things of life and to the standards of hospitality that prevailed among his class.

In the White House, Jackson lived and entertained lavishly, but without the stiffness and cold formality that had marked the Monroes' tenure. Under Old Hickory, the White House was a gracious home in which visitors were warmly welcomed. Jessie Benton, a senator's daughter, recalled the mansion on the eve of one reception:

> The great wood-fires in every room, the immense number of wax lights softly burning, the stands of camelias. . . . After going all through this silent waiting fairyland, we were taken to the State Dining-Room, where was the gorgeous supper table shaped like a horseshoe, and covered with every good and

glittering thing French skill could devise, and at either end was a monster salmon in waves of meat jelly.

Jackson's official hostess was his niece Emily Donelson, whose husband served the President as private secretary. Not quite twenty-one when she undertook the duties of First Lady, Emily had auburn hair, hazel eyes, and, according to Martin Van Buren, an "unaffected and graceful" manner. She competently managed the mansion, with its eighteen servants, and she and her husband, their young children, and their host of young friends and relations filled the White House with laughter and life. A typically domestic evening was described by a visitor:

> There was light from the chandelier, and a blazing fire in the grate; four or five ladies sewing around it. . . . Five or six children were playing about regardless of documents or work-baskets. At the farther end of the room sat the President in his arm-chair, wearing a long loose coat and smoking a reed pipe, with a bowl of red clay; combining the dignity of the patriarch, monarch, and Indian chief. Just behind was Edward Livingston, the Secretary of State, reading him a dispatch from the French Minister for Foreign Affairs. The ladies glance admiringly now and then at the President, who listens, waving his pipe towards the children when they become too boisterous.

Emily was very dear to Jackson, and she seriously displeased him in only one instance: she refused to welcome Peggy Eaton to the White House. The Eaton affair was a *cause célèbre* during Jackson's first term in office, and became something of an obsession with the President.

Peggy O'Neale, a pert, fair-skinned brunette, had met Jackson and his friend, Senator John Henry Eaton, when the two were guests at a hostelry owned by her father. Eaton and Peggy became close friends, although Peggy was married to a sailor named John Timberlake. When Timberlake later died at sea, ostensibly from tuberculosis, it was rumored that he had killed himself because of Peggy's involvement with Eaton. At Jackson's urging, Eaton had married Peggy soon thereafter.

All this had occurred prior to Jackson's inauguration. But when he made Eaton his Secretary of War, proper Washingtonians were horrified. The wives of Vice President John C. Calhoun and the other Cabinet members refused to meet Mrs. Eaton socially and snubbed her at every opportunity. Much to Jackson's displeasure, Emily Donelson also refused to receive Peggy, whom the President staunchly defended even when she was denounced by a group of clergymen. Obviously, the unfair gossip that had marred Rachel Jackson's life had been burned into her husband's memory, and the President was determined that another woman should not be made to suffer as his wife once had.

The Eaton affair was blown up out of all proportion, but it proved extremely useful to one person at least — Martin Van Buren, who had resigned the New York governorship to become Jackson's first Secretary of State. While the self-important ladies of the President's official family were boycotting the White House and Peggy, Van Buren — a widower, with no wife to worry about — championed Mrs. Eaton, even giving dinners in her honor. He won Jackson's gratitude and confidence, and he eventually devised a scheme by which

Jackson could purge the offenders: he himself would resign, thereby giving Jackson an excuse to disband his entire Cabinet. When Jackson started his second term in 1833, his new Vice President and heir apparent was none other than Martin Van Buren.

During Jackson's Presidency, the North Portico of the White House was finally built. It had been designed by Latrobe back in 1807, but not until Jackson's administration were funds available to construct it. (The South Portico had been erected in 1824.) Formal gardens were also created on the grounds, and iron pipes were laid to bring fresh water into the mansion. Previously two unsightly pumps had sent water into the house via open wooden troughs.

Jackson was allotted $50,000 to improve the interior of the White House. A fifth of that sum went to refurbish the East Room, which no doubt needed it after the inaugural festivities of 1829. Wood paneling and decorative wooden beams were installed there, and among the purchases were three cut-glass chandeliers, marble-top tables, Brussels carpets, new upholstery for the room's twenty-four armchairs and four sofas, and twenty spittoons. Jackson also bought a magnificent silver service from the Russian minister for $4,308, and a French dinner service and set of crystal with no fewer than nine sizes of wine glasses.

As his Presidency neared its end, Jackson's personal largess was curtailed by economic reverses. For two years in a row, the cotton crop at his Tennessee plantation, the Hermitage, had failed, cutting his income severely. Fewer guests were invited to the White House, and those who came were entertained less lavishly.

The gaiety of the White House was also diminished

because of the President's rapidly failing health. And then, late in 1836, came a shattering blow — Emily Donelson died of tuberculosis. Andrew Jackson, who had entered the White House a grief-stricken man, left it the same way.

His last public reception took place on Washington's birthday, February 22, 1837, just two weeks before his second term ended. An enormous cheese, weighing 1,400 pounds, had been presented to the President by the dairymen of New York, and the public was invited to help itself. In two hours, the huge cheese, four feet in diameter and two feet thick, was demolished. Jackson, supported by his son on one side and Jack Donelson on the other, came downstairs to greet his guests, but he was too weak to remain there for long. Few would have guessed that he had another eight years to live and would continue to influence national politics through those years.

Jackson was even more beloved by the people when he left the White House in 1837 than when he had entered it in 1829. But his handpicked successor, Martin Van Buren, did not fare as well.

Jackson had greatly expanded the power of the Presidency by his forceful actions on behalf of the federal union and the common man. His fight against the hated National Bank and his refusal to accept the southern opinion that a state could nullify a federal law are two cases in point. But Van Buren proved to be weak in the exercise of power. He was a superb politician, with a reputation for unmatched cleverness, as such nicknames as "the Red Fox" and "the Little Magician" imply. But he lacked charisma, and he was unable to alleviate the economic depression that

plagued the nation and undermined his own popularity.

Since Van Buren was a widower, with four unmarried sons, the White House lacked a hostess at the beginning of his administration. The void was soon filled, however, by Angelica Singleton, a lovely brunette from South Carolina. Her cousin Dolley Madison, abhorring a marital vacuum, introduced Angelica to Van Buren's son Abraham, and soon the White House had a young and charming hostess.

Probably because of the depression, Van Buren entertained chiefly at small dinner parties, featuring fine food prepared by his English chef. To some observers, however, Van Buren's tastes and manners were too refined for the Chief Executive of a democracy. His edict that the White House would not be open at all hours to uninvited guests offended many Americans, and Angelica unwittingly revived memories of Elizabeth Monroe by having butlers formally announce the arrival of visitors and by receiving guests while seated on a raised platform.

Van Buren had been one of the architects of Jackson's 1828 campaign strategy, which presented Old Hickory as the idealistic, fearless frontiersman engaged in battle with the corrupt, jaded establishment. The tables were turned on Van Buren in 1840 by the Whigs, who used the same approach but carried it much further. Their candidate, General William Henry Harrison, was actually a Virginia-born aristocrat, but he was presented to the voters as a backwoodsman who had been born in a log cabin and who drank hard cider, a man's drink — not the outlandish French wines favored by Van Buren, whose personal tastes and way of life

were pilloried as decadent and effeminate.

The tone for the campaign was set in April of the election year when Congressman Charles Ogle of Pennsylvania delivered a memorable address that has come to be known as "the gold spoon speech" because of its reference to gold spoons allegedly bought by Van Buren for the White House. Ogle's speech, a masterpiece of its kind, filled thirty-two pages in the Congressional Record. Comparing the President to emperors and kings, Ogle launched into an attack on the White House:

. . . let us enter his palace, and survey its spacious courts, its gorgeous banqueting halls, its sumptuous drawing rooms, its glittering and dazzling saloons, with all their magnificent and sumptuous array of gold and silver, crimson and orange, blue and violet, screens of Ionic columns, marble mantels, with Italian black and gold fronts, gilt eagle cornices, rich cut glass and gilt chandeliers . . . .

Actually, Van Buren had spent only $30,000 to refurbish the mansion, less than most of his predecessors. But that made no difference to Ogle, who held Van Buren personally responsible for everything in the mansion. Condemning the President for spending seventy-five dollars to have the famous thirteen-foot-long Monroe centerpiece regilded, Ogle also blasted him for spending thousands on a sterling silver-plate-and-gilt dessert set, bought from a Russian nobleman, which sounds suspiciously like the service bought by Jackson in the previous administration. To Ogle it was the kind "used in the palaces of kings and at the castles of the wealthy noblemen in Europe."

Ogle went on to accuse the President of using finger bowls, of loving "tassels, rosettes, and girlish finery,"

The fields between the Capitol and the White House were rapidly filling up with houses when the engraving at left was made in 1840. The view from the top of the South Portico, looking straight up Pennsylvania Avenue, shows the Capitol dome of 1825–56. Clark Mills's spirited equestrian statue of Andrew Jackson (right, below), was unveiled in 1853 in Lafayette Square, north of the White House. It was cast from cannon taken in the War of 1812.

of wearing cologne, and of sleeping late in the morning:

It was but a few days ago that an honest countryman, on his way to the fishing landings, after breakfast, having some curiosity to behold the magnificent "East Room" with its gorgeous drapery and brilliant mirrors, rang the bell at the great entrance door of the palace, and forthwith the spruce English porter in attendance, came to the door, and seeing that only "one of the people," "on foot," was there, slammed it in his face, after saying, "You had better come [later], the President's rooms are not open for visitors til ten in the morning." Whereupon the plain farmer turned on his heel, with this cutting rebuke, "I'm thinking the President's House will be open BEFORE DAY on the 4th of March for EVERYBODY; for OLD TIP [Harrison] is a mighty early riser, and was never caught napping — and doesn't allow serfs to be insolent to freemen."

Ogle's speech seems ludicrous today, but equating sophisticated tastes with "sloth and effeminancy" struck the right note for the America of 1840. The people turned out in large numbers to vote Van Buren out of office. "I put it to the free citizens of this country," Ogle had said. "Will they longer feel inclined to support their chief servant in a Palace as splendid as that of the Caesars, and as richly adorned as the proudest Asiatic mansion?" The answer, clearly, was no.

Van Buren made two unsuccessful attempts to recapture the Presidency. Then he retired, indulging himself in his taste for fine things without fear of political consequences and watching with a sad heart as his successors in the White House tried in vain to divert the American nation from its relentless march toward the tragedy of civil war.

III
The Lincoln Years

When James Buchanan turned the White House over to Abraham Lincoln in March 1861, he expressed to his successor the sense of relief that most outgoing Presidents have experienced: "If you are as happy, my dear sir, on entering this house as I am on leaving it and returning home, you are the happiest man in this country."

Lincoln's election had precipitated the secession of seven southern states and the specter of civil war haunted the nation — so the new Chief Executive was hardly a happy man on his inauguration day. But happiness had been rare in the White House for many years. A string of tragedies and bad luck had afflicted the seven families that had resided in the mansion between Van Buren and Lincoln; indeed, if a novelist tried to squeeze that much ill fortune into some multi-charactered piece of fiction, he would be criticized for an excessive and implausible concentration of woes. Life in the White House, however, was far stranger than fiction.

Twice in the 1840's, a President's body lay in the East Room. William Henry Harrison, Van Buren's successor and at sixty-eight the oldest man to take the presidential oath, insisted on delivering a two-hour inaugural address on March 4, 1841, despite freezing weather. He caught a chill, developed pneumonia and died within a month — the first President to die in office. Nine years after Harrison's death another former general, Zachary Taylor — whose campaign horse, Old Whitey, grazed on the White House lawn to the delight of visiting children — died in office, of acute gastro-enteritis after eating raw fruit and quaffing cold liquids on a sizzling July day.

Death also claimed a First Lady during these years. Letitia Tyler, wife of the Virginian who succeeded Harrison, died early in her husband's Presidency. An invalid, she had seldom left her room in the White House. Coincidentally, three other first ladies of the period were also unable to fulfill their functions as official hostess. Mrs. Taylor and Mrs. Millard Fillmore were both in very poor health. And Mrs. Franklin Pierce never overcame the grief that followed the death of her young son, Bennie. He had died in a railroad accident between Pierce's election in November 1852 and his inauguration the following March, and the melancholy lady had come to regard the tragedy as the price extracted by God for her husband's success. While Mrs. Pierce remained in her room, writing notes to the dead boy and asking servants to attend church for her sake, her aunt Mrs. Abby Kent Means served as hostess for her. One White House visitor remarked that "everything in that mansion seems cold and cheerless. I have seen hundreds of log cabins which seemed to contain more happiness."

The only President between Van Buren and Lincoln whose term in office is regarded by historians as successful was James Polk of Tennessee, a strong executive who, because he was a protégé of Andrew Jackson, was sometimes called Young Hickory. Polk, who was elected in 1844, oversaw the war with Mexico, a conflict that many Americans — including a first-term congressman from Illinois named Abraham Lincoln — condemned as immoral. But during Polk's administration, more than a million square miles were added to the United States. Polk worked so hard that he literally wore himself out. He refused nomination to a second term and

W. H. Harrison

Tyler

Polk

Taylor

Fillmore

Pierce

Buchanan

Lincoln

died only three months after leaving office. His wife, Sarah, had tried in vain to ease his burden by serving as his private secretary. A true puritan, Sarah had irked Washington by banning cards, dancing, and wine in the White House.

For Washingtonians who longed for gaiety and glamour in the Executive Mansion, there were only two bright spots in the twenty years prior to the Civil War. In 1844, the last year of his Presidency, the widower John Tyler married lovely Julia Gardiner of New York, who at twenty-four was thirty years his junior. The vivacious and regal Julia adored being First Lady, and the sound of waltz music emanated from the White House frequently. One visitor described Julia, wearing a purple velvet dress with a long train and an elaborate headdress, greeting guests while surrounded by twelve "maids of honor."

The other fashionable hostess was Harriet Lane, who acted as First Lady for her uncle, James Buchanan, the only bachelor ever to serve as President. Miss Lane was attractive and likable, and she helped her uncle entertain graciously such guests as the Prince of Wales and the first party of Japanese ambassadors ever to visit Washington. But it was hard for even Miss Lane to impart much gaiety at a time when the Union was disintegrating and her uncle seemed powerless, or unwilling, to save it.

The Executive Mansion itself changed little during this era. Because Congress was hostile to Tyler, the legislators refused to appropriate money to keep up the mansion during his Presidency. One reporter mourned that the White House was sadly changed "since the days of yore: its virgin white sadly sullied — its beautiful

pillars . . . besplattered with saliva of tobacco . . . the gorgeous East Room reflecting, from its monstrous mirrors, patched carpets . . . the splendid drapery falling in tatters all around time's rude hand. . . ." The next First Family, the Polks, cared little for appearances, but they did order gas piped into the mansion for the first time. President Fillmore had a large hotel stove placed in the kitchen and installed the 1850's versions of central heating and modern plumbing. His wife, Abigail, a former teacher, was appalled to discover that there were no books in the house, and at her instigation Congress appropriated money for a small library. Under Buchanan, a large conservatory was added on the west side of the house, and some new furniture, including a rococo-revival suite for the Blue Room, was bought at last.

All in all, it was a dismal period in the history of the nation and of the White House. For the most part the presidents were mediocre men, chosen because their mediocrity made them relatively acceptable to both North and South. Almost all of them were overwhelmed by the burdens of their office.

Then came Lincoln. His term in office was also marked by personal tragedy: the death of a beloved son, the mental instability of his wife, and of course his own assassination. But Lincoln's strength and wisdom, his dignity and his immeasurable compassion, restored greatness to the Presidency. And the White House took on a new and indelible stature simply because Abraham Lincoln had lived there.

Like other new presidents before him, Lincoln was immediately harassed by office seekers. Supplicants came from all over the country to see him, and all were

able to enter the Executive Mansion. They lined up outside his office on the west end of the second floor (today that room is the Lincoln Bedroom) and sprang upon him as he walked to the family quarters. "Solicitants for office besiege the President," reported Secretary of State William Seward. "The grounds, halls, stairways, closets, are filled with applicants, who render ingress and egress difficult." More pressing problems demanded Lincoln's attention, but he knew that patronage was an integral part of the political system and he coped good-naturedly with the onslaught. When he contracted a mild case of smallpox in 1863, Lincoln remarked wryly that at last he had something he could give everybody.

The first critical question facing Lincoln was what to do about Fort Sumter, the federal fort in Charleston Harbor that was under siege by secessionist troops. Disregarding the advice of his Cabinet — Lincoln made it clear right from the beginning that he would make the decision as he saw fit, not on the basis of consensus — he decided to send provisions to the fort. But before the relief ships arrived there, Confederate guns fired upon the fort and forced its surrender. After that Lincoln felt that he had no choice; he called for mobilization and so did the South. The war that would claim 600,000 American lives had begun.

To John Hay, one of his private secretaries, Lincoln explained his view of the conflict:

For my part, I consider the central idea pervading this struggle is the necessity upon us of proving that popular government is not an absurdity. We must settle this question now, whether in a free government the minority have the right to break up the government

whenever they choose. If we fail it will go far to prove the incapability of the people to govern themselves.

This was Lincoln's credo, the guiding principle behind his every action. He led the nation in civil war not for the purpose of freeing the slaves — although he abhorred slavery — and not to punish or subjugate the South, but to save the Union and prove that democratic government was possible.

Lincoln was never a cool, detached commander in chief, maneuvering faceless troops in a distant war like chessmen on a board. Since Virginia had joined the Confederacy, the President could see rebel campfires from the White House at night. If he used a spyglass, he could see Confederate flags flying over Alexandria across the Potomac.

Late in May 1861, during the first year of war, Colonel Elmer Ellsworth, a young man who had studied in Lincoln's Illinois law office, led a party of troops to Alexandria and was shot to death. A grief-stricken Lincoln ordered that the funeral be held in the East Room. Thus right from the beginning of the war the White House and the Lincolns shared the personal sorrow that would strike thousands of the nation's families in the coming four years.

On several occasions, especially early in the war, the White House and the President himself seemed in danger of being captured. Such was the case in July 1861, after the first battle of Bull Run. Confident of a quick northern victory, congressmen and other Washingtonians had journeyed in a holiday mood to nearby Manassas, Virginia, to watch the first major battle of the war. The inexperienced Union Army was quickly and decisively routed. That night a stunned Lincoln

These sketches, and the one on page 46, are the work of Alfred R. Waud, an English illustrator whose drawings were the basis for engravings that appeared in Harper's Weekly. *Below, Waud has portrayed the funeral in the East Room of Colonel Elmer Ellsworth, a protégé of Lincoln and one of the early casualties of the war. (The President is seated at the foot of the coffin.) At right, at the upset first battle of Bull Run, Colonel Ambrose E. Burnside leads green Rhode Island volunteers in an attack.*

lay on a couch in the White House, unable to sleep, as frightened civilians milled along Pennsylvania Avenue in a heavy rain. William Howard Russell, a British journalist, reported what he saw early that next morning in the capital:

> The rain was falling in torrents and beat with a dull, thudding sound on the leads outside my window; but louder than all, came a strange sound, as if of the tread of men, a confused tramp and splashing, and a murmuring of voices. I got up and ran to the front room, the windows of which looked on the street, and there, to my intense surprise, I saw a steady stream of men covered with mud, soaked through with rain, who were pouring irregularly, without any semblance of order, up Pennsylvania Avenue toward the Capitol. A dense stream of vapor rose from the multitude; but looking closely at the men, I perceived they belonged to different regiments, New Yorkers, Michiganders, Rhode Islanders, Massachusettsers, Minnesotans, mingled pellmell together. Many of these men were without knapsacks, crossbelts, and firelocks. Some had neither great-coats nor shoes, others were covered with blankets.

The Confederate Army did not follow up its great victory with a direct attack on Washington that day. But as Lincoln watched the retreating remnants of the Union force, he realized all too clearly that the war would be neither quick nor simple; it would be a long and dreadful conflict. Lincoln, who loved peace, was doomed to be a wartime President.

Because his generals proved to be either timid or inept, Lincoln was forced to become a military tactician; lights burned late in the Executive Mansion as the troubled President studied military textbooks. The office seekers gave way to people seeking pardons or promotions for their loved ones in the armies, favors and safe-conduct passes for themselves. Troops marched across the White House grounds; for a time, some were even quartered in the East Room. And each day the President read the latest casualty reports and grieved for his fallen countrymen.

Life in the White House settled down to a recognizable pattern. Lincoln rose early and put in at least an hour's work in his office before joining the family for breakfast at eight o'clock. A very light eater, he usually took only an egg and a cup of coffee. He then returned to his office for another hour's work before the influx of callers and petitioners, whom he saw from ten until one. First priority was given to Cabinet members and congressmen, then the public was admitted. His secretary and later biographer John G. Nicolay recorded one such presidential audience:

> Going into his room this morning to announce the Secretary of War, I found a little party of Quakers holding a prayer-meeting around him, and he was compelled to bear the affliction until the "spirit" moved them to stop. Isn't it strange that so many and such intelligent people often have so little common sense?

At one in the afternoon, Lincoln rejoined his family for lunch, which for him usually consisted only of a biscuit, a glass of milk, and sometimes a piece of fruit. Unless a Cabinet meeting or a reception was scheduled, Lincoln then returned to his office for another session of signing commissions, reading mail, writing speeches, and deciding whether or not to grant petitions. At

four, he usually went for a ride with his wife, often stopping at nearby hospitals to visit wounded soldiers. Dinner was at six, unless some official function had been scheduled.

If the pressures of office permitted, the President enjoyed spending the evening with his family, perhaps reading from Shakespeare or listening to his friend Ward Lamon sing such songs as "The Blue-Tailed Fly," a Lincoln favorite. Or he might attend the theater or a concert with his wife. More often, the President returned to his office to catch up on his paper work. Then he would walk across the lawn to the War Department, where he read the latest telegraph dispatches and learned the good or bad news of the day's fighting. When major battles were in progress, he often made several trips to the War Department, and stayed there into the early hours of the morning. But usually he returned to the White House and read for a while before retiring for the night.

John Hay reported that one night Lincoln, dressed for bed, came into the office to read to him and Nicolay an amusing episode from a book he had been reading. The President seemed "utterly unconscious that he with his short shirt hanging about his long legs, and setting out behind like the tail feathers of an enormous ostrich, was infinitely funnier than anything in the book he was laughing at."

Lincoln's wife, Mary, did all she could to ease his burden. She insisted that he go for a daily ride with her, brought him trays of food when he was too busy or worried to eat, invited to the mansion old friends whom she hoped would cheer his day. But she too was under great pressure. A Todd of Kentucky by birth

("One 'd' is good enough for God," Lincoln had quipped, "but not for the Todds"), Mary had nevertheless found herself scorned by the *grandes dames* of Washington society. Those with southern sympathies regarded her as a turncoat, married to a northerner who was an unpolished rustic as well. Northerners, on the other hand, saw Mary as a supporter of the rebels, and as the war progressed she was pilloried in the press as a spy and a traitor.

Nearly everything Mary Lincoln did seemed to bring criticism down upon her. If she gave parties, she was accused of being heartless in wartime. If she eschewed entertainments, she was told that she was not performing her duties as First Lady. It was certainly true that Mary was unwise, allowing herself to be used by unscrupulous favor seekers. But despite an uneven temperament, she was a loving wife and mother and most of the criticism directed against her in those troubled years was unfair.

One job that Mary accepted with enthusiasm was the redecoration of the White House. She liked nothing better than spending money, so she was delighted when Congress appropriated $20,000 to refurbish the mansion. The official rooms were "bare, worn, and spoiled," one witness reported, and looked like "the breaking up of a hard winter about a deserted farmstead." In many rooms the upholstery was frayed, the carpets were full of holes, the paint was peeling off the walls.

Under Mary's direction, the house was transformed. Velvet wallpaper from Paris was hung in the East Room, and on the floor was placed "the most exquisite carpet. . . . Its ground was of pale sea green, and in effect it looked as if an ocean, in gleaming and trans-

The miniature at left, portraying a tender moment between Lincoln and his son Tad, was painted in 1864 by Francis Bicknell Carpenter and includes a view, through the window, of the North Portico of the White House. In the lithograph portrait of the Lincoln family below, Tad is the child at Mrs. Lincoln's knee. Robert and Willie, who died in the White House, stand behind the table. The remodeled Capitol dome, completed in December 1863, appears in the background.

parent waves, were tossing roses at your feet." Swiss lace curtains, French draperies, and new satin and velvet upholstery completed the metamorphosis of the room. The other official rooms were also redone. Especially lovely was the state guest room which, according to Benjamin Thomas, Lincoln's distinguished biographer, "was resplendent with light-purple wallpaper figured with gold rose trees, and a bed canopy of purple silk trimmed with gold lace." The Lincolns' own living quarters were redecorated with expensive draperies and damasks. Only the President's simply furnished office, its walls adorned with military maps and a painting of Andrew Jackson, escaped Mary's hand.

Merchants from New York to Paris were delighted by Mary's buying sprees, but she soon discovered to her horror that she had exceeded the appropriation by $7,000. Lincoln was furious — how, he wondered, could any carpet be worth $2,500? — but he eventually agreed to ask Congress to pay the extra amount, and the lawmakers generously did so.

The newly decorated house was much admired during a large reception held on the evening of February 5, 1862. Contrary to tradition, guests were admitted by invitation only ("I don't fancy this pass business," Lincoln said). According to Ben Perley Poore, Mrs. Lincoln greeted her guests "in a white satin dress with low neck and short sleeves. It was trimmed with black lace flounces, which were looped up with knots of ribbon, and she wore a floral head-dress which was not very becoming." Lincoln, as usual, towered above the crowd and seemed uncomfortable in gloves and dress clothes. The Red, Green, and Blue rooms were open, as was the East Room, and all were filled with flowers.

The Marine Band played as the guests passed from room to room.

The schedule called for the State Dining Room to be opened at eleven. But the steward misplaced the key, which occasioned many jocular remarks about "forward movements" and "advance to the front" from the military men among the guests. At last the key was found. Ben Perley Poore described the scene:

The table was decorated with large pieces of ornamental confectionary, the centre object representing the steamer "Union," armed and bearing the "Stars and Stripes." On a side table was a model of Fort Sumter, also in sugar, and provisioned with game. After supper promenading was resumed, and it was three o'clock ere the guests departed. The entertainment was pronounced a decided success, but it was compared to a ball given by the Duchess of Richmond, at Brussels, the night before Waterloo. People parted there never to meet again.

Predictably, the affair was roundly criticized by journalists who felt that such lavish entertainments were out of place in wartime. "The Queen Must Dance" was the title of one article written by a reporter who did not know that the reception had been held at the urging of Secretary of State Seward. Nor did he know that for Mary and the President the evening had been tense and joyless. Their two younger sons were very ill, and Willie in particular was in great danger.

Willie and Tad Lincoln were the first children to live in the White House since Tyler's term sixteen years earlier, and even in the most sober of times they made the mansion ring with laughter and lightened their father's heart. Willie was a handsome, bright,

and affectionate eleven-year-old; Tad, three years younger, was gay and mischievous and spoke with a charming lisp. The entire White House was their playground. The mansion's flat roof became a battleship for them to command; the offices were romping rooms for their pet goat, Nanko, and the numerous other animals that made up their menagerie. Discovering the main controls for the mansion's bell system in the attic, the boys sent the servants scurrying by pulling various ropes. Once young Tad ate all the strawberries that had been purchased for a state dinner. And on one occasion, a Zouave doll, threatened with execution for having fallen asleep on sentry duty, was saved by the following written pardon: "The Doll Jack is pardoned by order of the President. A. Lincoln."

The February 5 reception had been scheduled before the boys had fallen ill, and since they seemed to be recovering, it was not cancelled. But the Lincolns' thoughts that evening had been of Willie, not their guests. Five days later Willie died, a victim of typhoid. Lincoln came into Nicolay's office and said, "Well, Nicolay, my boy is gone — he is actually gone!" The President then burst into tears and left the room. Later that day, servants found him lying in bed with Tad, whom he was trying vainly to comfort.

Lincoln's grief was immeasurable but he maintained control of himself. Mary, on the other hand, let herself go completely. She was unable to attend the funeral in the East Room, and her weeping and hysteria persisted for so long that Lincoln warned her she might have to be institutionalized if she could not restrain herself.

Ironically, not even the death of her child won Mary public sympathy. At a time when thousands of mothers were losing their sons in battle, her display of sorrow seemed excessive. As usual, she found relief in spending money. "I want you to select me the very finest and blackest and lightest long crepe veil," she wrote to a merchant, "and bordered as they bring them. Please get me the finest that can be obtained. Want a *very, very* fine black crepe veil, round corners and folds around. . . . I want the genteelest and tastiest you can find and have made." In the next two years, Mary ran up enormous clothing bills. When Lincoln sought reelection in 1864, Mary was terrified that he would lose and her creditors would immediately bill him for her outstanding debts, which by then had reached a grand total of $27,000.

Inconsolable, Mary banned the Marine Band concerts that had been held regularly on the South Portico of the White House and she forbade the use of flowers in the mansion. She refused to enter the rooms in which Willie's body had lain, and she turned to spiritualists in the hope of contacting his spirit. More than once, an incredulous Lincoln attended a séance with her. When Mary's half sister visited the White House in 1863, Mary told her that Willie's spirit came to her bedroom every night and stood at the foot of her bed.

In subsequent months Mary became increasingly temperamental and unpredictable; she also suffered from constant headaches. Vicious rumors circulating in the press did not help to alleviate her condition: she was insane, they reported; she was a spy; she had Negro blood. A member of the White House staff explained why she grew so unpopular:

It was not easy at first to understand why a lady who could one day be so kindly, so considerate, so gener-

Gen Hooker   Presd Lincoln

Presd Lincoln reviewing the Army of the Potomac on monday ptst.

*Lincoln, who often paid closer attention
to the war than many of his generals, is
shown (left, above) reviewing the Army
of the Potomac and (left, below) visiting
General George B. McClellan at his
headquarters at Antietam. The South's
vituperative reaction to the wartime
President is reflected in the cartoon at
right. A satanic Lincoln, surrounded by
demons and using the Constitution as a
footstool, composes the Emancipation
Proclamation, presumably paving the
way for the kind of bloody slave uprising
depicted in the painting on the wall.*

ous, so thoughtful and so hopeful, could upon another
day appear so unreasonable, so irritable, so despon-
dent, so even niggardly, and so prone to see the dark,
the wrong side of men and women and events.

Eventually, Mary discovered that visits to nearby
hospitals took her mind off her own sorrows. She nursed
wounded soldiers regularly, and her presence was
greatly appreciated by those who benefited from it.

In addition to the weight of his office, his own grief
over Willie's death, and his concern for Mary, Lincoln
worried about young Tad, now totally dependent on
his father. A lesser man would have broken under the
strain, but Lincoln somehow found the strength to
endure his private and public·ordeals.

Month after month passed without any news to cheer
the North. Then, in September 1862, the bloody battle
of Antietam was fought. If it was not a clear-cut victory
for the Union, at least it was not a defeat of the kind
that had been occurring with such dismal regularity.
Lincoln took this opportunity to issue the Preliminary
Emancipation Proclamation, which announced that in
three months all slaves in rebel territory would be
freed. Although he had been under great pressure from
abolitionists to take such action, he knew that if the
North did not win the war, the decree was as enforce-
able in the South as "the Pope's bull against the
comet!" But the quasi-victory at Antietam allowed him
to issue it from a position of strength.

True to his word, he signed the final proclamation
on January 1, 1863. The annual New Year's reception
was held in the White House that morning, and after-
ward the President repaired to his office with about a
dozen government officials. But he paused before sign-

ing the historic document. "I have been shaking hands
since nine o'clock this morning and my right arm is
almost paralyzed," he said. "If my name ever goes down
in history it will be for this act and my whole soul is
in it. If my hand trembles when I sign this Proclamation, all who examine the document hereafter will say,
'he hesitated.' " After a few moments, Lincoln signed
the Emancipation Proclamation with a steady hand.

In mid-1863, the first really decisive northern victories occurred at Vicksburg, Mississippi, and Gettysburg, Pennsylvania. Lincoln was jubilant. Ulysses S.
Grant, the victor at Vicksburg, was the general Lincoln
had long been searching for — one whose deeds equaled
his promises.

That fall, the President accepted an invitation to
speak at the dedication of the Gettysburg cemetery.
Although Tad was ill, Lincoln went to Pennsylvania on
November 19, 1863, and delivered a simple speech, 286
words long, that will be remembered as long as democracy endures. The crowd seemed far more appreciative,
however, of a florid two-hour oration given by Edward
Everett. "The cheek of every American must tingle
with shame," said the *Chicago Tribune* of the Gettysburg Address, "as he reads the silly, flat, and dishwatery
utterances of the man who has to be pointed out to
intelligent foreigners as the President of the United
States."

That same month, Grant won another great victory
at Chattanooga, Tennessee, and the following March
he came to the White House to be named general in
chief of all the Union armies. But despite Grant's abilities, more months of indecisive fighting and heavy
losses lay ahead. Lincoln followed each contest closely.

Ulysses S. Grant, newly appointed general in chief of the Union armies, is greeted by Lincoln at an 1864 reception in the East Room of the White House (below, left). Chandeliers similar to the one in the background of the painting have always been an important feature of the East Room, giving it a sense of lofty elegance befitting the grand receptions, balls, and concerts that have been held there. At right, in a photo taken in the present-day East Room, a delicate cut-glass chandelier in the Empire style is reflected in a pair of opposed mirrors.

During the long and bitter battle of the Wilderness, in May 1864, he "scarcely slept at all," according to artist Francis Carpenter, who met the President in the main hall of the domestic apartments of the White House. Carpenter later described Lincoln:

> . . . clad in long morning wrapper, pacing back and forth a narrow passage leading to one of the windows, his hands behind him, great black rings under his eyes, his head bent forward upon his breast, — altogether such a picture of the effects of sorrow, care, and anxiety as would have melted the hearts of the worst of his adversaries, who so mistakenly applied to him the epithets of tyrant and usurper.

No amount of rest could relieve what Lincoln came to refer to as "the tired spot" within him.

As generals Grant and William Tecumseh Sherman began to move against the South in a giant pincer movement, it became clear at last that the Confederacy was doomed. In November, Lincoln was narrowly reelected for a second term. Crowds carrying banners and lanterns swarmed across the White House lawns the night after the election, and Lincoln spoke to them from a window of the mansion:

> We can not have free government without elections, and if the rebellion could force us to forego, or postpone a national election, it might fairly claim to have already conquered and ruined us. . . . But the election, along with its incidental, and undesirable strife, has done us good too. It has demonstrated that a people's government can sustain a national election, in the midst of a great civil war. Until now it has not been known to the world that this was a possibility.

The next day, in the presence of his Cabinet, Lincoln

opened an envelope that he had sealed months earlier. "This morning, as for some days past," he had written, "it seems exceedingly probable that this Administration will not be reelected. Then it will be my duty to so cooperate with the President elect, as to save the Union between the election and the inauguration; as he will have secured his election on such ground that he cannot possibly save it afterwards."

The election reminded Lincoln of a dream he had had on the eve of his first election in 1860. In a large looking glass he had noted two distinct images of himself, one imposed upon the other. One image was much paler than the other, however. Lincoln had told Mary about the dream, and she had pessimistically interpreted it to mean he would be elected to a second presidential term but would not live through it.

Beloved by much of the nation, Lincoln was also vilified more viciously than any other President had been. Detested by the South, he was also condemned by abolitionists, who thought he had done too little for the Negro, and by some northern whites, who thought he had done too much. Obviously, there were thousands of people who would have liked to see Lincoln dead. One night in 1862, he had actually been shot at; the bullet had missed him but had knocked off his hat. Yet the precautions taken to protect him were erratic at best. This was partly Lincoln's own fault; he fatalistically believed that his life could not be protected from a determined assassin, and he thought it unseemly for the head of a democracy to be constantly surrounded by troops or guards. Nevertheless, new precautions were taken after the election of 1864. No longer did the President go alone to the War Department at night,

and extra troops were assigned to the White House.

A month after Lincoln's second inauguration in March 1865, the President had another disturbing dream. In it he heard weeping, rose from his bed, and went to the East Room. There he saw a corpse laid out on a catafalque, surrounded by troops and mourners. When he asked who the corpse was, he was told that the President had been murdered.

On the night of April 11, crowds again massed at the White House. Robert E. Lee had surrendered to Grant at Appomattox Court House two days earlier, and the jubilant throng expected to hear words of victory from their President. Instead, he urged compassion and reconciliation. "Finding themselves [the Confederate states] safely at home, it would be utterly immaterial whether they had ever been abroad," he said. "Let us all join in doing the acts necessary to restoring the proper practical relations between these states and the Union, and each forever after, innocently indulge his own opinion whether, in doing the acts, he brought the States from without into the Union, or only gave them proper assistance, they never having been out of it." Tad Lincoln laughed as each page of the speech was read and allowed to drop into his hands. But Lincoln was deeply disturbed by the crowd's subdued reaction to his plea of forgiveness. It must have been all too clear to the President that binding the wounds of war now that peace had come would be even more difficult than winning victory.

But Lincoln did not live to press his policy of reconciliation. He was struck down on Good Friday by an assassin's bullet, and early on the morning of April 15, 1865, he died.

For the first time, the White House received the body of a murdered President. Mourning thousands came to view the corpse, which lay on a black-draped catafalque in the East Room, just as Lincoln had dreamed. Then the President's body, and Willie's were returned to Springfield, along the same route both had followed to the first inaugural only fifty months earlier.

"Now," Secretary of War Edwin M. Stanton had said, at the moment Lincoln died, "he belongs to the ages." Stanton was right. Abraham Lincoln was America's most noble son, an inspiration to all subsequent occupants of the White House, who have aspired to but never achieved his greatness.

IV
Presidents in a Gilded Age

Very few people understand to what straits the President's family have been put at times for lack of accommodation. Really, there are only five sleeping apartments, and there is little privacy."

Mrs. Benjamin Harrison's complaint of the early 1890's was a familiar one; it had been echoed by each new resident of the White House as surely as spring had followed winter. And yet nothing had been done to alleviate the situation. The First Family's living quarters and the President's offices were still jammed together on the mansion's second floor, an arrangement that allowed adequate space for neither. And the lack of privacy was still appalling. The White House was open to visitors daily, and office seekers, cranks, and the merely curious had no difficulty making their way upstairs from the official rooms on the first floor.

Several first ladies had suggested, in desperation, that the presidential family move to some other residence, using the White House only for official entertaining. That idea had never been seriously considered, however, probably because no President had wished to incur the wrath of traditionalists who viewed the White House as a symbol of national continuity. Nor did anything come of the many schemes for enlarging the Executive Mansion.

The most elaborate plan was espoused by the exasperated Mrs. Harrison herself, whose White House entourage consisted of a married son and daughter and both their families, as well as an assortment of other relatives, and who therefore acutely felt the need for additional space. In 1891 the First Lady and her architectural advisers presented the following proposal: on the west side of the mansion, an "official wing" would be erected; it would be connected to the main house by a corridor and a rotunda filled with statuary. Balancing this structure on the east would be the "national wing," containing historical art. At the southern end of the White House grounds, a long conservatory would be built; it would have round palm houses at either end, echoing the two rotundas of the new wings. A large courtyard would thus be formed, and in it would be built a fountain commemorating Columbus's discovery of America and the laying of the White House cornerstone some three hundred years later.

"The entire tour of this uninterrupted series of salons, anterooms, corridors, rotundas, conservatories, and winter garden . . ." wrote one expert on architecture after seeing the plans for Mrs. Harrison's proposal, "would afford for the comfort and enjoyment of the throng of distinguished guests a promenade of 1,200 feet from point of departure, making the entire circuit, thus avoiding the confusion of returning by the same way."

The scheme might have been enacted had the President not incurred the wrath of "Czar" Thomas Reed, the all-powerful Speaker of the House. Because Harrison had crossed Reed on the matter of a minor appointment, Reed blocked the White House bill and refused to let it come to a vote. A disappointed Carrie Harrison had to content herself with minor improvements to the mansion, such as the laying of new floors to replace rotting old ones and the installation of electric lights and bells. It took four months to electrify the old mansion, and the Harrisons were reportedly quite leery of the new convenience; they often left lights burning all night rather than risk shocks by turning them off.

Grant

A. Johnson

Hayes

Garfield

Cleveland

Arthur

McKinley

B. Harrison

Mrs. Harrison, who fell ill of pleurisy and tuberculosis during the last year of her husband's Presidency and died in the White House, is credited with one positive achievement: starting the White House china collection. Because she loved to hand-paint china herself — she decorated hundreds of items, ranging from pitchers to her grandson's porcelain bathtub, and even held a class on china painting in the White House — she was distressed to learn that the china of previous administrations had not been preserved. Under her guidance representative pieces from the past were located and gathered together in the White House.

Mrs. Harrison's sense of history was unusual for the era; in the post-Lincoln years there was little respect for tradition. Each new occupant redecorated the White House to his own taste, and the belongings of his predecessors were usually discarded or stored away and seldom cherished.

Indeed, when Lincoln's immediate successor, Andrew Johnson, moved his family into the White House in 1865, he found it almost bare. During the five weeks between Lincoln's death and his family's departure from the mansion, souvenir hunters had roamed the building without restraint and had removed everything that could be carried away, from expensive silver ornaments to pieces of furniture. By the time the Johnsons arrived, the place was a shambles.

Like a number of other first ladies, Johnson's wife was an invalid, and she left her official duties to her daughter, Martha Johnson Patterson. Martha was charming and efficient. With a limited budget she refurbished the mansion simply and pleasantly. She also bought two Jersey cows which she kept on the

White House grounds, assuring her family of fresh milk and butter.

Her father's Presidency, which began during the deep mourning over Lincoln's death, had a glorious moment on May 23 and 24, 1865, as 200,000 victorious Union troops passed in review up Pennsylvania Avenue before returning to civilian life. "The reviewing stand, erected on a sidewalk in front of the White House, was a long pavilion, with a tight roof, decorated with flags and bearing the names of the principal victories won," recorded Ben Perley Poore. Flanking the President were generals Grant and Sherman and the members of the Cabinet. Stands on either side of the pavilion were occupied by other officials, ladies, and wounded soldiers; and on the other side of the avenue, the members of Congress were seated.

It must have been thrilling to watch the jubilant Union soldiers march by their new commander in chief. Lincoln was gone, of course, but the White House symbolized his key role in the great victory that had been won after four bloody years. "The Army of the Potomac was six hours in passing the reviewing stand," Poore wrote. "As each brigade commander saluted, President Johnson would rise and lift his hat." The next day the Division of the Mississippi passed along the same route. "Their faces were finely bronzed," Poore tells us, "and they marched with a firm, elastic step that seemed capable of carrying them straight to Canada, or by a flank movement to Mexico in a short space of time."

That day of triumph was soon forgotten, however, as Johnson's Presidency degenerated into a struggle between himself and the Radical Republicans in Congress. The congressional leaders disapproved of his benevo-

Carrie Harrison, who cuts a formidable figure in Daniel Huntington's portrait at right, had elaborate plans for enlarging the White House. But when these were scuttled by Congress, she was forced to indulge her fine sense of taste and history on a smaller scale. Her lasting contribution to White House tradition is the china collection she started. Today, every President is represented in it. Examples from six administrations are shown opposite, including (second from top) the china Mrs. Harrison herself designed.

lent policies toward the defeated South and tried to deny Johnson his constitutional powers as Chief Executive. When Congress passed a law making it illegal for a President to remove his appointees from office without legislative approval, the battle reached a climax. Johnson defied the new law, and was swiftly impeached by the House of Representatives.

The Senate trial of Andrew Johnson dragged on for two months — perhaps the most tense two months in White House history. The President did not attend the trial, but he directed his defense from the Executive Mansion, following each day's events carefully. "The White House was the scene of endless legal conferences," writes historian Milton Lomask. "Many a quiet Washington dawn found Martha Patterson . . . brewing coffee and tea in the kitchen while Johnson and his lawyers polished off a night-long session in the big oval library on the second floor."

The final vote in the Senate was thirty-five against Johnson, nineteen for him; but since a two-thirds majority was required for a conviction, Johnson was acquitted. He and the nation were the winners; the power of the Presidency as an independent branch of the government was upheld. That night, according to one Washingtonian, the White House was "as hilarious as a royal palace after a coronation."

Despite his vindication, Johnson never seriously considered running for reelection; he and everyone else knew that General Grant, easily the most popular man in the nation, was going to be the next President.

When Grant moved into the mansion in 1869, the first thing he did was to dismiss the military guard that had been posted there since the beginning of the Civil

Monroe

Lincoln

B. Harrison

T. Roosevelt

Truman

L. B. Johnson

War. It was, he seemed to be saying, a new era, with past conflicts laid to rest. But Grant proved to be far too weak an executive to lead the country effectively. He deferred constantly to Congress and to his own ill-chosen advisers, and he surrounded himself with cronies who took advantage of his trust in them to feather their own nests. A series of scandals rocked the country during his eight years in office, and although Grant's personal honesty was never impugned, it was all too clear that his superb battlefield judgment did not carry over into civilian life. "I never wanted to get out of a place as much as I did to get out of the Presidency," he said later, adding his voice to the chorus of former presidents — especially in the years immediately preceding the Civil War — whose ambitions brought them to an office that was too large for them to fill.

Grant's wife, Julia, on the other hand, came to love being First Lady, even though she never was able to convince Grant to let her have her cross-eyes straightened out. (The President liked her that way, he said firmly.) "My life at the White House was like a bright and beautiful dream," she said in retrospect, "and we were immeasurably happy. . . . Life at the White House was a garden spot of orchids, and I wish it might have continued forever, except that it would have deterred others from enjoying the same privilege."

She had felt quite differently about the mansion when Grant was first elected. Regarding it as dingy and inadequate, she had hoped to continue living in her I Street residence. When that proved impossible, the good-natured Julia decided to make the best of it, and proceeded to put her own stamp on the mansion.

The Grants were the First Family during the period

Under the Grants the White House became the center of a sparkling social life. The strain of war had lifted and Mrs. Grant, wearing satin and lace in the photo at right, could pamper herself with fine clothes and elegant furnishings. In 1873 the East Room, shabby from long neglect, was fitted with gilt-encrusted pillars and beams and extravagantly decorated in what has been called "steamboat-palace" décor (below). There, dressed in a shower of lace, the Grants' daughter, Nellie, was married before the glittering audience of socialites and dignitaries seen at far right.

that has come to be known as the Gilded Age. Vast fortunes were acquired by self-made men who lived lavishly and ostentatiously. The Grants, essentially unsophisticated people, were impressed by wealth but unable to distinguish between the elegant and the vulgar, and the White House reflected that common failing of the time.

The most extensive refurbishing took place in 1873, after an engineer's report on the condition of the mansion revealed that the timbers were rotten, the cellars damp, and the ceilings cracked. "It hardly seems possible to state anything in favor of the house as a residence," the report said. "One large ceiling fell last year, but fortunately when the room was unoccupied. . . ."

As redecorated under the Grants, the Executive Mansion was all gilt and cut glass and heavy beams and columns. Everything was overdone and tasteless, and the rooms looked more like steamboat salons than state apartments.

The East Room, redone in what the Grants called "Greek style," was probably the ugliest of all. But it was there that the Grants received with pride the two hundred guests invited to the wedding of their daughter Nellie in 1874 — the most publicized nuptial in years. Nellie, a vivacious eighteen-year-old, had met Algernon Sartoris, an Englishman, on shipboard while she was returning from a trip abroad. The Grants reluctantly gave their consent to the match and invited their friends to a wedding that the newspapers referred to as "quiet and unostentatious."

Flowers "filled the windows, festooned the walls, wreathed the columns, covered the mantels and tables, hung from the chandeliers, and formed arches in the doorways," one account of the East Room ceremony tells us. The Marine Band played for the guests until the ceremony itself began. Then, under a huge wedding bell made of roses, the couple was wed. Nellie's gown, it was reported, contained four thousand dollars worth of Brussels lace.

After the 11 A.M. ceremony, a wedding breakfast was served in the State Dining Room. The menu, printed on white satin, included the following:

Soft-Shelled Crabs on Toast. Chicken Croquettes with Green Peas. Lamb Cutlets with Tartare Sauce. Aspic of Beef Tongue. Woodcock and Snipe on Toast. Salad with Mayonnaise. Strawberries with Cream. Orange Baskets Garnished with Strawberries. Charlotte Russe. Nesselrode Pudding. Blancmange. Ice Cream Garnished with Preserved Fruits. Water Ices. Wedding Cake. Small Fancy Cakes. Roman Punch. Chocolate. Coffee.

Gifts to the bride, in addition to Grant's own $10,000 check, included such tokens as a $4,500 dinner service, a $500 handkerchief, and a $1,000 ring.

With Nellie married (it was not, sad to say, a happy marriage, and the couple eventually separated), the Grants wound up their second term in accustomed style. The President continued to make frequent use of the billiard table he had had installed, and to spend a great deal of time in the White House stables, where his beloved horses were kept. Lavish entertainments remained the rule: the Grants loved them, the press loved them, and the *nouveau riche* who lionized the Grants loved them too.

It was a relatively quiet affair, however, that took place on Saturday evening, March 3, 1877. Thirty-six

Rutherford and Lucy Hayes, who posed for the photograph at left on their wedding day in 1852, created a sober and homey atmosphere at the White House — to the dismay of Washington's more exuberant social circles. The engraving at right portrays a typical evening's entertainment: the President (seated at the table) and his family and friends gathered round to hear Carl Schurz, the Secretary of the Interior, at the piano. The annual Easter egg-rolling contest on the White House lawn, a tradition begun by Lucy Hayes, is depicted in the watercolor shown at right, below, which was done some years after the Hayes administration.

guests gathered in the White House for a dinner honoring the new President-elect, Rutherford B. Hayes. But before the dinner began, Grant, Hayes, and Chief Justice Morrison Waite slipped into the Red Room where Hayes quietly took the presidential oath of office.

Grant's term officially ended that Sunday, but since no oaths could be administered on the Sabbath, Hayes was not due to be sworn in until Monday. Because Hayes had just recently been declared the winner in a contested election, it was deemed dangerous to leave the nation officially without a Chief Executive, even for a few hours. So Hayes was sworn in secretly; he took the oath again, as scheduled, during the public ceremonies on Monday.

Like Grant, Hayes came from Ohio. But unlike their predecessors, the members of the new First Family believed in living simply and were not impressed by vulgar displays of wealth.

Lucy Hayes, the first First Lady to have attended college, became known as Lemonade Lucy because of a rule forbidding all wines and spirits in the White House. Actually, the rule was her husband's idea and was reportedly promulgated after an unpleasant incident involving too much drinking at an affair early in Hayes's single term. Nevertheless, the diplomatic corps and the rest of official Washington were dismayed at the prospect of having to endure interminable state dinners without the aid of alcoholic beverages. "Buttermilk flowed like water," cracked one wag after a reception, and James A. Garfield, then a congressman, was heard to complain about "a State dinner at the President's wet down with coffee and cold water." Unknown to the President and his wife, a sympathetic steward would alleviate the guests' sufferings by spiking the Roman punch, a sherbetlike concoction that was made of lemon juice, sugar, and egg whites. Served at mid-meal as a refresher, the Roman punch course became known as "the Life-Saving Station." The Hayeses never caught on.

Always an individualist, Mrs. Hayes found the White House perfectly livable. "No matter what they build, they will never build any more rooms like these!" she told a friend while showing her around the mansion. It was Mrs. Hayes who began the tradition of Easter egg rolling on the White House lawn each year.

On a typical day, Hayes rose at seven, had breakfast at half-past eight, and then said morning prayers with Lucy and the children. Meetings and office work occupied him until two, when he lunched, after which, dressed in silk hat and frock coat, he went for a ninety-minute carriage ride. He napped before dinner and if possible spent his evenings with the family. A favorite recreation was sitting around the piano with Lucy, the children, and family friends, singing old favorites. Official receptions were held when necessary, and the Hayeses presided over them graciously. But promptly at 10 P.M. the band played "Home Sweet Home" as a signal to the guests that the evening was concluded.

In December 1877 the Hayeses celebrated their twenty-fifth wedding anniversary by repeating their original vows before a group of their closest friends and relatives; Lucy even wore the gown she had been married in. It was surely one of the most sweetly sentimental moments in White House history.

During the Hayeses' occupancy, telephones were installed in the White House, and so was a telegraph

machine. But the First Family itself remained very much a product of old-fashioned America, in the most complimentary meaning of the term.

Their successors, the James Garfields, were also a happy, uncomplicated couple. But their stay in the mansion was destined to be brief and tragic. In June 1881, three months after Garfield had been inaugurated, the First Lady fell ill of malaria and almost died. Then, on July 2, the President was shot by a disgruntled office seeker. The bullet lodged in his back muscles, but without the use of X-ray machines, the doctors could not tell if it had come to rest in a vital organ. They probed and prodded in vain, unable to locate the bullet.

For weeks, the President lay upstairs in the White House, his strength waxing and waning. The nation was informed of every change in his pulse beat, every minor symptom. "I should think the people would be tired of having me dished up to them in this way," Garfield himself remarked, but the public's appetite for such news was insatiable.

Medical experts today believe that the bullet, which soon became encysted, would have caused no serious trouble if left alone. But the doctors continued their probing, worsening the infection and sapping Garfield's strength. Alexander Graham Bell came to the White House once with a new electric device designed to find the bullet, but his attempt, like all the others, was unsuccessful.

In September the President, at his own request, was moved by train to the New Jersey seashore, where it was hoped that the ocean air would aid his recovery. But the nation's vigil, and Garfield's long, painful

The elegant austerity of the Cross Hall, looking toward the East Room, is shown in the contemporary photograph at right. Eighteenth-century cut-glass chandeliers are supplemented by Empire-style torchères; the entrance to the Blue Room is at right, between the flags. In 1882, President Arthur installed a Louis Tiffany stained-glass screen between the pillars to shelter the Cross Hall from the main Entrance Hall, as seen in the period photograph reproduced at left.

ordeal, ended on September 19, 1881, when the President finally died.

Garfield's Vice President, dapper, portly Chester Alan Arthur, was a far cry from the plain, bearded men who had occupied the Executive Mansion with their unglamorous wives in recent years. Arthur sported luxuriant muttonchop whiskers, and he led a far more elegant life than had his predecessors. As a matter of fact, he refused to move into the White House until it had been completely redecorated. It looked, he said, like a "badly kept barracks."

With absolutely no regard for the past, Arthur had twenty-four wagonloads of old furniture and clothing removed from the mansion's storerooms and auctioned off. They included such disparate items as Abigail Adams's portmanteau, a sideboard that had belonged to Lucy Hayes, a pair of Lincoln's pants, and some mattresses from the Buchanan administration. According to some accounts, furniture dating from the times of Monroe and Jackson was also sold.

Under Arthur's patronage, the New York artist and decorator Louis Comfort Tiffany transformed the old mansion into an *art nouveau* palace. New bathrooms and an elevator were installed, but those amenities seemed far less important to the new President than the decor. Each evening, Arthur visited the White House to check on Tiffany's progress.

The public rooms were all completely redecorated. The Blue Room was painted a soft robin's-egg blue, "with ornaments in a hand-pressed paper, touched out in ivory, gradually deepening as the ceiling was approached." A frieze, depicting eagles and flags, graced the Red Room. The East Room walls were painted

white, its ceiling silver. Separating the hallway between the East Room and the State Dining Room from the outer vestibule was Tiffany's *pièce de résistance*, "the opalescent glass screen . . . which reached from the floor to the ceiling, [and] had . . . a motif of eagles and flags, interlaced in the Arabian method." A small dining room was Arthur's particular concern. Looking forward to many intimate, elegant dinners, he had the room hung with heavy gold paper, with pomegranate-red plush draping the windows and fireplace. Throughout the house, everything that could be sprayed with gold, was; everything that could be overstuffed, was; and every space that could hold a potted plant, held two.

President Arthur deemed the mansion fit to inhabit in December 1881; he moved in with a French chef, a personal valet (who preferred to be called a "messenger"), and his sister, who served as hostess for the Chief Executive, a widower.

In addition to furnishings, clothing, and food, Arthur was very particular about flowers. He enlarged the conservatories, and state functions during his administration were always marked by ornate floral arrangements. At one dinner, for instance, the centerpiece was four feet long and a foot and a half high, and was christened the Swinging Gardens of Babylon.

Arthur's love of elegant living, coupled with his refusal to discuss his personal life with reporters, resulted in many critical articles that labeled him a fop. Actually, Arthur was a far better President than had been expected. Ennobled by his office, he turned his back on the cronies who had been expected to rule him, and he worked harder than his life-style would seem to indicate.

The beautifully decorated East Room, President's Mansion, Washington, D. C.
Copyright 1901 by Underwood & Underwood.

Blue Room in President's Mansion, Washington, D. C.

Red Room in President's Mansion, Washington, D. C.

Swamped by a tide of flowers, festoons, and potted palms, bedecked with multipatterned rugs and wallpapers, hung with weighty chandeliers, and crammed with massive settees, the White House was never as oppressively decorated as in the 1880's and 1890's. From the top, the stereoscopic views at left are of the East Room, the Blue Room, and the Red Room. The bachelor Grover Cleveland, one of those who aspired to the privilege of living in these forbidding chambers, won the Presidency in 1884 despite the fact — trumpeted in the cartoon at right — that he had reportedly fathered an illegitimate child.

Meanwhile, he added a new cachet of stylishness to Washington. "I dined at the President's Wednesday," wrote one lady. "The dinner was extremely elegant, hardly a trace of the old White House taint being perceptible anywhere, the flowers, the damasks, the silver, the attendants, all showing the latest style and an abandon in expense and taste."

Gossips frequently linked Arthur with some eligible lady or other, but all the stories proved untrue. It was his successor, Grover Cleveland, who thrilled America's romantics and delighted the Washington press corps by getting married in the White House, the first and only Chief Executive ever to do so.

Cleveland, a husky, mustachioed New Yorker, had won election in 1884 even though the opposition had branded him as the father of an illegitimate child. Most politicians would have denied the unprovable accusation, but the always honest Cleveland admitted that he had known the child's mother, and that he might be its father. To the credit of the voters, they admired Cleveland's openness — as opposed to the evasiveness of his opponent, James G. Blaine, who had been mixed up in some shady financial deals — and voted for him anyway. Cleveland thus became the first Democratic President elected in twenty-eight years, breaking the string of Republican chief executives stretching back to Lincoln's time. (Andrew Johnson, a Democrat, had been elected Vice President in 1864 on a fusion ticket with Lincoln.)

In the first months of his Presidency, Cleveland's sister Rose served as his hostess. A former teacher, lecturer, and essayist, she was a formidable lady who allegedly survived the boredom of large receptions by silently conjugating Greek verbs. Cleveland himself kept no personal servants, and although he retained Arthur's French chef, he hated fancy food. "I must go to dinner," he once wrote. "I wish it was to eat a pickled herring, Swiss cheese and a chop at Louis' instead of the French stuff I shall find."

For years Cleveland had been enamored of Frances Folsom, the daughter of his late law partner. He waited until she had graduated from college and then asked her to marry him. The tall, lovely brunette — not quite twenty-two when she married Cleveland on July 2, 1886 — was to prove an invaluable social and political asset to her forty-nine-year-old husband. Washington was beside itself with excitement over the prospect of a new First Lady.

Only close friends, relatives, and members of the Cabinet received invitations to the ceremony, written in Cleveland's own hand: "I am to be married on Wednesday evening at seven o'clock at the White House to Miss Folsom. It will be a very quiet affair and I will be extremely gratified at your attendance on this occasion."

John Philip Sousa conducted the Marine Band, clad in scarlet and gold, as the guests arrived for the ceremony. The Blue Room was bedecked with pansies and roses, and candelabra given to the White House by Andrew Jackson softly lighted the room. When the simple ceremony was over, church bells rang out, a twenty-one-gun salute was fired at the nearby Navy yard, and the large crowd that had gathered on the White House lawn cheered the newlyweds. The reception took place in the State Dining Room. "The decorations were of an elaborate character," according to Ben

Perley Poore. "A mirror in the centre of the table represented a lake, on which was a full-rigged ship, made of pinks, roses, and pansies. The national colors floated over the mainmast, and small white flags, with the monogram 'C.F.' in golden letters, hung from the other masts."

The Clevelands' honeymoon was marred by over-zealous reporters, but the marriage was a happy one and Frances was enormously popular. White House receptions drew up to eight thousand guests, each wishing to shake the hand of the glamorous young First Lady. On one occasion, Mrs. Cleveland had to have her arm massaged before she could resume greeting her guests.

It was during Cleveland's first term that Frank G. Carpenter, a correspondent for the *Cleveland Leader*, told his readers what it was like to visit the White House. The Tiffany screen in the vestibule reminded Carpenter "of the jeweled mosaic walls of the Potsdam palace of Frederick the Great, which cost a fabulous sum and which was built to blind the eyes of the other monarchs of Europe to the actual slender state of his purse." The walls of the East Room, which he described as the largest parlor in the United States, were:

. . . of embossed paper of white and gilt, and the ceiling, beautifully finished in oils, is three times as high as that of an ordinary house. From its richly decorated beams hang enormous chandeliers, each one of which is made up of six thousand pieces of Bohemian glass, and cost five thousand dollars. When the chandeliers are lighted, the eight massive mirrors, set into the walls of the vast room, reflect the brilliant lights, which bring out the richness of the old-gold satin furniture and the beauty of the soft mosslike carpet.

After commenting favorably on the portraits of first ladies and presidents in the various parlors, Carpenter then described the conservatory:

. . . palm trees, orchids and ferns, roses of a hundred varieties, lemon and orange trees bloom away while the wintry winds blow outside and the temperature stands at zero. During receptions, the guests wander with oh's and ah's into this tropical paradise, meeting at intervals the guards who keep watchful eyes upon their fingers.

Amidst all the magnificence, Carpenter pointed out, there was still much that was commonplace:

. . . and in spots it is actually shabby. As we came up through the handsome portecochere, we looked over the iron railing and saw the President's servants ironing his nightshirts and other unmentionable garments in the laundry of the basement. . . . Even in the fine mosaic vestibule, we found a mixture of the grand and the cheap. Two rough door mats lie upon the rich mosaic floor. The varnish is cracked upon the grained woodwork, and beside the door leading to the second story is a walnut umbrella stand that would be dear at five dollars. The hall and the stairs that brought us to the President's offices are covered with an old piece of Brussels carpet which was good once, but which has been patched, sewed, and resewed. It would not bring fifty cents at auction.

One of the hardest-working presidents, Cleveland labored long and late in his office, toiling at a desk that had been presented to the White House by Queen Victoria during the Hayes administration. It was made from the timbers of the *Resolute*, a ship that had been sent by the British to the Arctic to rescue Sir John

The first and only President's wedding held at the White House, Grover Cleveland's marriage to Frances Folsom in 1886 (depicted in the engraving at left), took place in the Blue Room, the "elliptic saloon" of James Hoban's original design. Handsomely furnished by President Monroe after the fire of 1814, the Blue Room was often redecorated but seldom improved upon during subsequent administrations. In 1962 it was restored, as seen in the photo at right, below, in a style befitting to the Monroe era. The Minerva clock (right), imported from France by Monroe, again graced the mantelpiece for which it was created. A decade later, in 1972, the room was again redecorated in an early-nineteenth-century style.

Franklin, leader of a lost polar expedition. The *Resolute* was abandoned but saved by American whalers, and the desk presented to Hayes as a token of Britain's gratitude.

The popular Frances Cleveland proved to be clairvoyant when she and her husband vacated the White House in 1889, to make way for the Benjamin Harrisons. "Now, Jerry, I want you to take good care of all the furniture and ornaments in the house," she said to a steward, "for I want to find everything just as it is now when we come back again. For we are coming back just four years from today." She was, of course, absolutely right. Harrison served one term and then, still grieving over his wife's death less than five months earlier, turned the mansion back to the Clevelands in March 1893.

Frances had given birth to a baby girl while Cleveland was between terms, and another daughter was born during his second administration. Because the public had free access to the White House grounds, the children's nurses had a great deal of trouble keeping gawking visitors from bothering them. One day, Mrs. Cleveland discovered to her horror that a crowd of tourists had taken one of the children away from the nurse, and was handing her around from one to another. The justifiably outraged First Lady ordered the gates to the Executive Mansion's grounds closed, but an unsympathetic public resented her action greatly.

Fear for the children's safety, and for that of Cleveland himself — he had received many threatening letters — caused the First Family to spend as much time as possible away from the White House. They bought a residence in the Washington suburbs for weekends,

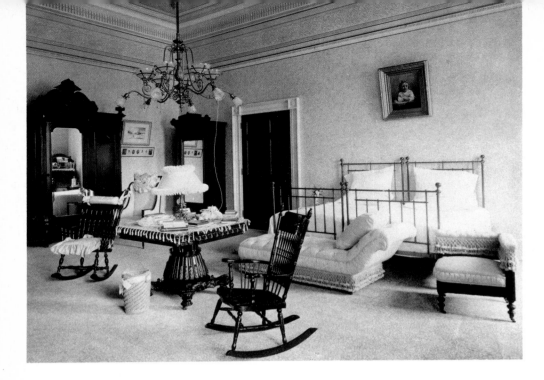

Dressed in summer lace and holding a single blossom, the tragic Ida McKinley posed in the White House conservatory for the haunting photograph at right. Frail and epileptic — and obsessed by the deaths of her two daughters — the First Lady spent most of her time in the room at left, crocheting bedroom slippers. The portrait above the twin beds is of Katie, the McKinley's elder daughter, who died in 1875 at the age of four and a half.

and they spent their summers in Maine. Like almost all other presidential families, however, the Clevelands came up with a plan for enlarging the White House; the scheme was not adopted, nor was the one approved by the next President, William McKinley.

Actually, the proximity of offices and living quarters in the mansion was an ideal arrangement for McKinley, who wished to remain as close as possible to his wife, Ida, still another in the string of invalid first ladies. An emotionally unstable epileptic, given to frequent, embarrassing seizures, Ida spent most of her time in her room on the northwest corner of the second floor, crocheting slippers by the score for friends, acquaintances, and charitable organizations. With his office just a few doors away, the President could visit her often and rush to her aid if she had an attack.

Much to the dismay of official Washington, Ida insisted on acting as hostess at state functions. It had always been customary for the President to be seated across from the First Lady at state dinners, thus creating four places of honor — two flanking the host, two the hostess. McKinley, however, insisted on having Ida next to him, which resulted in many problems of protocol. Foreign guests in particular were critical of this breech of established etiquette. And time after time at dinners or receptions, White House guests looked on in bewilderment or horror as the President, always alert to the first signs of an oncoming seizure, threw a napkin or handkerchief over the First Lady's face. Sometimes she resumed normal conversation after a few minutes; at other times she had to be helped from the room and taken to her quarters. At large public receptions, Ida was usually given a nosegay to hold and was seated on a chair near her standing husband. Unable to shake hands, she nodded politely to her guests, who were whisked by to the next person in the reception line.

McKinley's unfailing devotion to his wife won him widespread admiration — the popular Chief Executive easily won election to a second term in 1900 — but Ida's condition weighed heavily upon him. Certainly he had problems enough without that extra burden. His Presidency was marked by a war with Spain and a long insurrection in the Philippines.

After war broke out in 1898, twenty-five telegraph wires and fifteen telephone wires were hooked up in one of the small second-floor offices, which became a communications center known as the War Room. There, McKinley spent many hours, following the movements of American ships and troops in the Caribbean and Admiral George Dewey's fleet in the Pacific. Later, when the war was won and the fate of the Philippines was in question, McKinley spent hours studying the islands on wall maps, and wondering if the United States had the right to take control of them.

"I walked the floor of the White House night after night until midnight," he said later, "and I am not ashamed to tell you . . . that I went down on my knees and prayed Almighty God for light and guidance more than one night. And one night late it came to me . . . that there was nothing left for us to do but take them all, and to educate the Filipinos, and uplift them and civilize them and Christianize them. . . ." The Filipinos — Christianized long before by Spain — looked at the matter in a somewhat different light, however, and the result was an insurrection that lasted three years and cost the lives of a thousand American soldiers.

Having resigned as Assistant Secretary of the Navy to fight in the Spanish-American War, Theodore Roosevelt became a national hero when he led his Rough Riders up San Juan Hill in 1898, a scene recreated in the detail below from Frederic Remington's painting. Elected governor of New York later that year, T.R. became the reluctant candidate for Vice President on the McKinley ticket in 1900. His subsequent domination of that campaign is the butt of the cartoon at left, in which the war hero — his belt stuffed with press notices — gives the dwarfed President a ride on the pommel of his saddle. At right, the last posed photograph taken of McKinley shows him at the Pan-American Exposition in Buffalo, New York, on September 5, 1901, the day before he was shot by Leon Czolgosz.

At the White House, meanwhile, battles of a far more trivial nature were being fought. Addison Porter, the President's pompous secretary, and Captain Theodore Bingham, the mansion's majordomo, worked together behind McKinley's back to make the White House a social center for the elite, to the total exclusion of the average citizen.

It was true that far too many people jammed into the White House each time there was a public reception. Three or four thousand guests passed through the Blue Room during a typical affair. Poles had to be erected in the basement to hold the floor up, and so great was the crush that ladies fainted with alarming frequency. Some evenings the situation was so bad that guests who lifted their hands up for some reason, found that they were unable to lower them; gentlemen often found themselves pressed up against ladies in a most embarrassing fashion. All this just to shake the President's hand, glance at the distracted First Lady, and drink a glass of ice water — the only refreshment served at these functions!

Porter and Bingham suggested limiting the number of invitations to receptions to one thousand, and the President agreed. But he objected to their efforts to keep gate-crashers away. Ladies, the aides complained, had found their own servants at the receptions. Prostitutes mingled with high society. "The greater part of these people," Bingham wrote, "have been such as butchers, cabmen, market and grocery clerks, and the scum of the city." Essentially kind and democratic, McKinley would have no part of the scheme to keep the hoi polloi away. Later, when Porter and Bingham sent a notice to the newspapers announcing that only

men in evening dress and ladies without bonnets would be welcomed at the mansion's receptions, a furious McKinley put an immediate end to the restrictions.

On several occasions, friends of the President had spoken to him about the loose security precautions at the White House. An assassin could easily gain access to the President's private quarters, and at the crowded receptions, McKinley was an easy target. When a rash of political assassinations swept Europe, the President's intimates finally persuaded him to accept an additional bodyguard. McKinley remained fatalistic, however, and went out without a Secret Service attendant whenever possible.

It was not at the White House, but at a reception at the Pan-American Exposition in Buffalo, New York, that the worst fears of the President's intimates were finally realized. A deranged anarchist, Leon Czolgosz, fired two shots at McKinley, and the President died of his wounds a week later, on September 14, 1901. His last words, whispered to Ida, were from his favorite hymn, "Nearer, my God, to Thee, Nearer to Thee."

Twelve hours later, Vice President Theodore Roosevelt, summoned to Buffalo from an outing in the Adirondacks, took the oath as the twenty-sixth Chief Executive. "Now look," exclaimed Senator Mark Hanna of Ohio, a close adviser of McKinley who had fought against giving Roosevelt the vice-presidential nomination in 1900, "that damned cowboy is President of the United States."

V

Bully Pulpit, Shrouded Sickroom

Perhaps others have lived longer in the place and enjoyed it quite as much," Theodore Roosevelt said about the White House, "but none have ever really had more fun out of it than we have." Like a cool breeze after an oppressive hot spell, the rambunctious Roosevelts replaced the childless McKinleys in the Executive Mansion and transformed it into a home overflowing with love and laughter.

Not quite forty-three when he took office in 1901, Roosevelt is the youngest man in American history to become President. His seemingly limitless energy, enthusiasm, and self-confidence ideally suited a nation that had only recently become a major world power and was somewhat intoxicated by its own importance and potential. Edith, T.R.'s cool, efficient wife, was a flawless First Lady, and the six Roosevelt children were as uninhibited and healthy a brood as any parents could have desired.

Alice, the seventeen-year-old daughter of T.R.'s brief first marriage — his wife had died of Bright's disease two days after their only child's birth — was soon dubbed Princess Alice by the press and became the most publicized presidential daughter since Nellie Grant. Her irreverent and unpredictable behavior, which included sliding down banisters and carrying a snake in her purse; her incredibly full social schedule; and her real charm and vivaciousness made her the delight of newspapermen, hostesses, and Washington's bachelors. "I can be President of the United States or I can control Alice," the exasperated Roosevelt once said. "I cannot possibly do both."

The rest of the children were equally incorrigible. Theodore Jr., who was fourteen at the time T.R. was sworn in as President; Kermit, twelve; Ethel, ten; Archie, seven; and Quentin, four, were totally unimpressed by the fact that the White House was a national shrine; to them, it was simply a wonderful place to live. They borrowed large metal trays from the kitchens and slid down the staircases on them. They crawled along the spaces between ceilings and floors, and rode on roller skates and bikes and walked on stilts all through the mansion. Each of the circular seats in the East Room, Alice later recalled, had "an elevation in the center, out of which sprouted a potted palm. When the palms were removed, a not-too-large child could crouch in the vacant space and pop out at passersby."

Only occasionally did a child really step out of line and have to be punished. The President related one such incident:

I have just had to give [Quentin] and three of his associates a dressing down. Yesterday afternoon was rainy, and four of them played five hours inside the White House. They were very boisterous and were all the time on the verge of mischief, and finally they made spitballs and deliberately put them on the portraits. I did not discover it until after dinner, and then pulled Quentin out of bed, and had him take them off all the portraits, and this morning required him to bring in the three other culprits before me. I explained to them that they had acted like boors; that it would have been a disgrace to have behaved so in any gentleman's house, but that it was a double disgrace in the house of the Nation; that Quentin could have no friend in to see him, and that the other three could not come inside the White House, until I felt that a sufficient time had elapsed to serve as punish-

T. Roosevelt

Taft

Wilson

ment. They were four very sheepish boys when I got through with them.

On another occasion, after Quentin and his "White House gang" had launched an attack on the nearby War Department Building, T.R. sent him this note: "Report to me at the White House immediately for you know what."

Obviously, the President could be a stern disciplinarian when necessary. But accounts of life in the White House show that he was a loving father who, despite a usually frantic schedule, managed to spend a great deal of time with the children. In a letter to Kermit, then away at school, he recounted the evening routine with the two youngest boys:

The last two or three nights I have had terrific pillow fights with Archie and Quentin. Quentin's idea is to get as many pillows as possible in a heap and then lie on them apparently on the theory that he is protecting them from me. This enrages Archie, who addresses him with lofty contempt as "kid," and adjures him to stand up manfully and "fight the bear." If mother is tired I usually read to them, but if I cannot then Archie solemnly reads aloud to Quentin. To-day, for our sins, Archie has a mask and a tin horn with which he runs about, armed with divers wooden swords and spears, to assail the policemen, ushers, and even me in his capacity as dragon.

Edith Roosevelt was fond of saying that she really had five boys, meaning of course that the President was in many ways still a child. He exercised strenuously every day and expected those who worked for him to be as fond of athletics as he was. Tennis, medicine ball, football, and every other sport was played on the White House grounds, and wrestlers and boxers came frequently to the mansion to demonstrate their skills and engage the President in combat. For a time, T.R. was fascinated by jujitsu. Once he staged a match between an American wrestler and a Japanese jujitsu expert; the American was declared the winner of the impossible contest, a decision that naturally pleased the unabashedly chauvinistic Roosevelt. On another occasion, some fifty or sixty guests were invited to the East Room to watch two Chinese wrestlers perform. The event did not delight Mrs. Roosevelt, who was equally disinterested in some film footage of fighting wolves that the President managed to obtain and insisted on showing at the White House.

When the President injured his leg in an accident and was consequently unable to exercise in his usual ways, he devised a sport called "singlestick" to keep in shape. He described the game to Kermit:

But at six every evening, General Wood comes over and we play at singlestick together. We put on heavily padded helmets, breastplates and gauntlets and wrap bath towels around our necks, and then we turn to beat one another like carpets. Now and then by accident one or the other of us gets hit where there is no protecting garment. We are not very good at it yet and consequently are able to hit far better than we parry. Ted insists that each one simply "swats" the other in turn like the medieval "biding a buffet." But it does give me some exercise which I should not otherwise get. We look like Tweedledum and Tweedledee — Alice Through the Looking Glass.

Probably because of his own sickly childhood — he suffered from asthma and poor eyesight and was

83

taunted as a sissy until he learned to fight back — T.R. was totally intolerant of the weak. Once, when a woman suggested that his children might get hurt during a strenuous football game, the President replied coldly, "I would rather one of them should die than have them grow up weaklings." (Ted and Kermit, who overheard his remark, told him solemnly the next day, "Father, we have consulted together as to which of us must die, and we have decided that it shall be the baby.")

T.R. always demanded even more of himself than he did of others, however. He was determined to be a strong Chief Executive, and he brooked interference from no one, not even influential members of his own party in Congress, as he wielded the big stick at home and abroad. Prosecuting trusts, dealing firmly with a coal miners' strike, fighting for the conservation of natural resources, he tried to use his office to bring about a "square deal" for all Americans.

He was equally energetic in his conduct of foreign relations. When Colombia, of which Panama was then a part, refused to cooperate in the building of a canal, T.R. acquiesced in — if he did not engineer — a revolt of the Panamanians, who declared their independence and almost simultaneously agreed to let the United States build a canal across the isthmus. A few years later, when Congress was hesitant in voting funds to send the Navy around the world — T.R. felt that the Great White Fleet was a graphic representation of American power and would help keep peace — the President said that he had enough money to get the fleet to the Pacific; and if Congress failed to appropriate additional funds, the fleet would just have to stay there.

To Roosevelt the White House was a "bully pulpit," from which he could preach his ideas and values. On a practical level, however, it was far too small to accommodate both his large family and the executive offices. And thus in 1902 the long-urged renovation and enlargement finally took place.

The First Family moved to a house on Lafayette Square as workmen, under the supervision of the architectural firm of McKim, Mead & White, tore the mansion apart and put it back together again. The operation had five stated goals: to make the White House structurally sound again; to move the President's offices out of the main building and thereby give the family more room; to arrange for the more efficient handling of crowds at official receptions; to enlarge the State Dining Room; and to remove the unsightly appendages that had been built onto the house over the years. All these aims were accomplished, as the President had insisted, in a manner that was in keeping with the building's original style and with the ideas of its original architects.

Removing the tangle of greenhouses that had obscured Jefferson's terrace on the west side of the mansion, the architects erected a new executive wing, connected to the mansion by a colonnade built on the old terrace. The new wing was one story high and built of white brick; it contained an office for the President, a Cabinet room, a press room, and other badly needed offices and facilities. On the east side of the house, where Jefferson's other terrace had once stood, a porte cochere was built, enabling invited guests to emerge from their carriages during inclement weather without getting wet. A complex of rest rooms and cloakrooms

WHITE HOUSE.
WASHINGTON. *June 22d 1904*

Darling Ethel,
Here goes for the picture letter!

Ethel administers necessary discipline to Archie and Quentin.

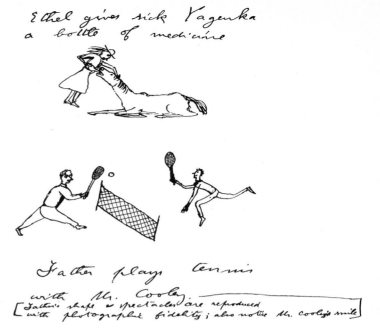

Ethel gives sick Yagenka a bottle of medicine

Father plays tennis with Mr. Cooley.
[*Father's shape & spectacles are reproduced with photographic fidelity; also notice Mr. Cooley's smile*]

was also created on the mansion's east side.

The mansion itself, which President Roosevelt officially renamed the White House — dropping the more formal Executive Mansion from official stationery — was renovated from top to bottom. Modern plumbing, wiring, and heating were installed, and the unsafe floors, which had had to be shored up during large receptions, were rebuilt. The west staircase to the executive offices, no longer needed, was removed, permitting the enlargement of the State Dining Room. No longer would the President have to entertain large groups in the cross hall, protected from drafts only by the Tiffany screen — which, by the way, was another casualty of the renovation. Removed from the enlarged State Dining Room were two exquisite mantels originally made for Hoban; they were installed in the Red and Green rooms, where they became focal points of the new decor. The design for the new mantel in the State Dining Room showed lions' heads at either end. T.R. looked at the design, ruled out the lions, and suggested an American animal, the buffalo.

The florid Victorian interiors of past administrations gave way, for the most part, to a simpler and more classic style. True, white bear rugs — reflecting Roosevelt's passion for hunting — lay on the floors of the Blue and Green rooms for a brief period, but in many respects the rooms were attractively redone. The Blue Room, for instance, harked back to the French Classical style of the Monroe period; the furniture was white and gold, with blue and gold upholstery, and the walls were hung with "heavy, corded blue silk, on which is embroidered at top and bottom the Grecian fret," according to the architect's report. In the Green Room,

"the wall covering and curtains of green velvet are copied from an old piece of Genoese velvet; the marble console table shares with the mantel the distinction of age and grace; the furniture — upholstered in tapestry — the rugs, the mirror, the andirons, the crystal chandelier and sidelights, all are new."

Handsomest of all was the East Room, again as described in the architect's report:

The walls of the East Room are covered with wood paneling, enameled; the ornamental ceiling is done in stucco, and set in the walls are twelve low relief panels by Piccirilli Brothers, sculptors, the subjects being taken from Aesop's fables. On each the east and west sides of the room are two mantels of colored marble, with mirrors over them and candelabra on the shelves. . . . The window draperies are of heavy yellow silk damask; the banquettes are gilded and carved and are covered with silk velours, and there are four new console tables with marble tops. In this room, as in the other rooms on the drawing-room floor . . . hardwood floors have been laid, and wainscots have been introduced, of which the lower member has been made of marble of suitable color.

Upstairs, the old offices were transformed into bedrooms and baths. No longer would the First Family have to encounter clerks, office seekers, and politicians as they passed from one room to another. At last the second floor became a relatively private home. It had cost Congress $65,000 for the executive wing and $475,-000 for the renovation of the mansion, but all future first families would be grateful that the money had been appropriated.

As Roosevelt had insisted, all the new construction

With his children Roosevelt was an eager playmate, always ready to lead them on a hike or join them in a pillow fight before bedtime. His letters to them were laced with humor, and when they were small he sent them "picture letters" like the one opposite addressed to twelve-year-old Ethel. Below, a beaming Roosevelt appears in the battered slouch hat he habitually wore on the campaign trail.
 Overleaf:
In the East Room, the scene of Alice Roosevelt's wedding in 1906, Martha Washington's portrait complements the Gilbert Stuart portrait of her husband (shown on page 28) which hangs nearby.

complemented the original structure. "The White House is the property of the nation," he had said, "and so far as is compatible with living therein it should be kept as it originally was. . . . It is a good thing to preserve such buildings as historic monuments, which keep alive our sense of continuity with the nation's past." Keenly cognizant of the mansion's history, T.R. was especially aware that Lincoln had lived there. His Secretary of State, John Hay, had been Lincoln's private secretary, and when T.R. was inaugurated for his own full term in March 1905, Hay gave him a ring containing hair that had been cut from Lincoln's head on the night of his assassination. "I think of Lincoln, shambling, homely, with his strong, sad, deeply furrowed face, all the time," the President wrote to a friend. "I see him in the different rooms and in the halls. For some reason or other he is to me infinitely the most real of the dead Presidents."

In February 1906 the White House was the scene of Alice Roosevelt's highly publicized marriage to Nicholas Longworth, an Ohio congressman who would become Speaker of the House in later years. Gifts poured into the mansion from friends, the public, and heads of state, including the Empress of China, who sent rolls of rare silks to the bride. Finally, the President announced that it would be improper for a daughter of a chief of state to receive such expensive gifts, and asked that no more be sent. "So like him to come to that decision after the gifts were on the way," commented his old friend Senator Henry Cabot Lodge. "At least, Theodore didn't issue his awful ban before the string of pearls from Cuba arrived," sighed his sister Anna Cowles.

It was the first White House wedding of a President's daughter since that of Nellie Grant, almost thirty-two years earlier. The house was bedecked with flowers, and a simple but lovely altar was erected in the East Room. The President was Alice's only attendant. After the ceremony, guests crossed the mansion to a reception in the State Dining Room, but Alice and Nicholas greeted their close friends in the private dining room; there Alice grabbed a sword from a friend wearing military dress and cut her wedding cake.

More than sixty years later, Alice Roosevelt Longworth was entertained at the White House by President Nixon, who showed her a recently acquired period print of her and her father descending the staircase on her wedding day. Mrs. Longworth did not hesitate to point out that the print was inaccurate — she and the President had come down from the second-floor family quarters in the White House elevator.

Time after time, Roosevelt told friends and relatives how much he and his wife loved living in the White House. In a letter to author Joel Chandler Harris, for instance, he discussed the children's current pets — which at the time included a terrier named Jack; Eli, a macaw; a Chesapeake Bay dog called Sailor Boy; Jonathan, the piebald rat; two kangaroo rats; a flying squirrel; and of course the famous pony Algonquin, whom the children once smuggled up in the elevator to visit a sick brother. To Harris the President also wrote:

Last night Mrs. Roosevelt and I were sitting out on the porch at the back of the White House, and were talking of you and wishing you could be sitting there with us. It is delightful, at all times, but I think especially so after dark. The monument stands up distinct

90

but not quite earthly in the night, and at this season [June] the air is sweet with the jasmine and honeysuckle.

Two years later, in the same vein, T.R. wrote to his eldest son:

I am having a reasonable amount of work and rather more than a reasonable amount of worry. But, after all, life is lovely here. The country is beautiful, and I do not think that any two people ever got more enjoyment out of the White House than Mother and I. We love the house itself, without and within, for its associations, for its stillness and simplicity. We love the garden. And we like Washington. We almost always take our breakfast on the south portico now, Mother looking very pretty and dainty in her summer dresses. Then we stroll about the garden for fifteen or twenty minutes, looking at the flowers and the fountain and admiring the trees.

Life in the White House was not always so serene, however. Edith never knew until the last moment whom the President would bring to lunch or dinner — the servants always had to be prepared for several unexpected guests — or whom he would ask to stay the night. Guests ranged from Buffalo Bill to conservationist Gifford Pinchot, from champion wrestlers to Booker T. Washington. The latter's presence at one meal caused a major sensation. T.R. had invited the noted Negro educator to the White House to discuss appointments to federal jobs in the South, and later — on the spur of the moment, according to one account — had asked him to stay on for dinner. The South was shocked at the news; the press there raved hysterically. The Memphis *Scimitar*, for instance, called it "the most

damnable outrage ever . . . when he invited a nigger to dine with him at the White House." Roosevelt announced that he would invite Washington to dine at the White House just as often as he pleased. But he was clearly taken aback by the unexpected uproar, which hurt the Republicans in the South in the next election, and he did not invite Washington or any other Negro to dine at the mansion again.

Edith Roosevelt's "female Cabinet" was far less controversial than the Booker T. Washington incident, but it was also an innovation. She invited the wives of Cabinet officers to join her weekly in the Green Room for a session of embroidery, knitting, and — according to the capital's grapevine — gossip. It was rumored that careers were advanced or stalled by what was said at these exclusive get-togethers. It may have been at one such session that Edith first heard of the extramarital love affair of a diplomat's wife. The always proper Edith dispatched presidential aide Archie Butt to warn the woman that unless she broke off her improper liaison she would not be invited to White House receptions. As T.R.'s military aide, Butt had to be ready for almost any assignment: on one occasion he had to join the President on a ninety-mile horseback ride, to prove that such a stint was not too rigorous a physical requirement for Army officers.

It was estimated that Edith Roosevelt presided at more than two hundred musicales, dinners, and receptions during her tenure as First Lady, and it has been said that during all that time she never made a social mistake. Crowds of up to eight thousand people flowed into the mansion, but Edith met all the demands made upon her with equanimity. To avoid shaking hands

with all those people, for instance, she held a bouquet of flowers while she stood in the receiving line — a practice that had been invaluable to poor Ida McKinley. "It is very interesting to see how wisely Mrs. R. segregates society in Washington and the wisdom she shows in sending her invitations," Butt wrote. "She has some entertainments in which the 'inner circle or smart set,' so called, predominate; then others when the political element is in the majority; others again when she invites only those whom she really likes and whose society she herself enjoys. The people invited do not know that they have been segregated in this fashion, but it has the effect of making her gatherings very pleasant for everybody."

To take as much worry as possible off his wife's shoulders, T.R. insisted that large state dinners be prepared by an outside caterer rather than in the White House kitchens. "Last year he got $10 a plate," Butt wrote in 1908, "but this past winter they cut him to $8. This includes all the wine with the exception of champagne. There is no entertainment fund, so you can see how rapidly the President's pay is eaten up."

Roosevelt was enormously proud of Edith. "She is so gracious and kind, and withal so careful that she has imparted to the White House much of herself. It is my wife," he said, "who often reminds me of some new struggling author and suggests that he be invited to visit us or to dine or lunch. She really knows the value of such things more than I do, I fear, and I often get the credit of doing things to which she is entitled."

Roosevelt could probably have been elected to another term of his own in 1908. Four years earlier, however, on election night of 1904, he had announced that

he would consider McKinley's unfilled term as his first and the term starting March 1905 as his second, and he had pledged to honor the anti-third-term tradition and not seek reelection. Although he and his family came to regret that promise, he could not retract it.

One evening during T.R.'s second term, William Howard Taft, the obese Secretary of War who was a close friend of Roosevelt, found himself alone with the President and Mrs. Taft in the second-floor library. Ensconced in an easy chair, the President shut his eyes and intoned: "I am the seventh son of a seventh daughter and I have clairvoyant powers. I see a man weighing three hundred and fifty pounds. There is something hanging over his head. I cannot make out what it is. . . . At one time it looks like the Presidency, then again it looks like the chief justiceship."

"Make it the Presidency," said Helen Taft.

"Make it the chief justiceship," said her husband.

The ambitious, imperious Helen Herron Taft prevailed. Taft became Roosevelt's handpicked successor and had no trouble beating two-time loser William Jennings Bryan in the 1908 election. The relationship between Taft and Roosevelt had already begun to sour by the following March, but into the White House nevertheless moved the Tafts, their three children (including future senator Robert A. Taft), the President's Filipino valet, and a cow named Pauline Wayne, the last cow to be kept by a First Family. Also moved in were Oriental rugs and teakwood furniture purchased by the Tafts during his tenure as governor of the Philippines, an enormous bathtub built especially for the outsize Chief Executive, and a Victrola, which was placed in the Blue Room. On more than one occasion,

Taft dozed away in his chair after dinner as his bored and embarrassed guests — not daring to leave without proper farewells — were treated to a Caruso recording punctuated by stentorian presidential snores.

Helen Taft purchased a fleet of automobiles to replace the horsedrawn carriages that had previously transported the Chief Executive and his family. And she shocked the Roosevelts by replacing the White House ushers with Negro servants in blue livery, who stood at the mansion's entrance and received guests' calling cards on silver trays.

For a few months, Helen Taft reveled in her position as First Lady. But then she suffered a stroke and was an invalid for many months. She recovered enough of her health to preside at White House functions later in Taft's term — more than four thousand guests attended a nighttime garden party, held in June 1911, to celebrate the Taft's silver wedding anniversary — but the realization of her longtime ambition to be First Lady brought neither her nor her husband the happiness she had expected. Taft split openly and bitterly with Roosevelt, who bolted the Republican party to run on the Progressive ticket in 1912, thereby dividing the G.O.P. vote and denying Taft reelection. Woodrow Wilson, governor of New Jersey and former president of Princeton University, was the winner. (Happily, Taft achieved *his* cherished ambition in 1921, when Warren Harding named him chief justice of the Supreme Court, a position he filled with distinction for nine years.)

For Wilson as for Taft, the joy of electoral victory would be followed by personal sorrow and political disappointment.

Seated on his old friend Roosevelt's shoulders, William Howard Taft wears the heir apparent's crown in the 1906 Puck cartoon at far left. An immense man, Taft weighed upwards of 300 pounds, and four men could fit into the special tub he had installed in the White House (left). But there was room for only one Republican candidate in 1912, and the split between Roosevelt and Taft paved the way for Woodrow Wilson's election. Below, the outgoing Taft and the incoming Wilson are shown, in a photograph from the Chicago Historical Society, riding in the 1913 inaugural parade. With them is Senator Murray Crane.

In 1913, during the Wilson family's first happy months in the White House, the vivacious and talented Wilson women devoted much energy to social work in Washington. In Robert Vonnah's group portrait at right Ellen Wilson is shown serving tea to her daughters, Margaret, Eleanor, and Jessie. When the First Lady died in 1914, she and her husband had been married nearly thirty years. Sir William Orpen's portrait of the President (left), now hanging in the East Wing entrance lobby, was painted in 1919 while Wilson himself was in France negotiating the Versailles treaty.

At first, though, the Wilsons were quite happy in their new home. The President, his wife, Ellen, and their three daughters, all single and all in their twenties, moved into the Executive Mansion gleefully. That first night, according to one witness, "there was a continuous running through the house, from one room to another, a shrill voice screaming to someone else as a new place was discovered." Jessie, Eleanor, and Margaret loved being escorted around town by handsome young officers, and they delighted in such pranks as joining a party of tourists in the mansion and making disparaging remarks about the First Family to scandalized visitors, who were unaware of their true identity.

The Wilsons enjoyed each other's company enormously, and preferred evenings *en famille* to entertaining guests. In the upstairs library, they played the piano and sang, read aloud to each other, or listened appreciatively as the President did his "imitations" — a talent that would have surprised official Washington. Included in Wilson's repertoire were imitations of a drunk, an Englishman, a villain, and a Fourth of July orator, as well as one of Theodore Roosevelt delivering an impassioned address. The President was also fond of limericks, the following being one of his favorites:

> There was a young monk of Siberia
> Whose existence grew drearier and drearier,
> Til he burst from his cell with a hell of a yell
> And eloped with the Mother Superior.

Ellen Wilson, the First Lady, was neither fashionable nor sophisticated, but she was a loving wife and mother. An artist by avocation, she turned one of the attic rooms into a studio. But much of her time was spent trying to alleviate in any way she could the conditions in Washington's appalling slums, which had come to her attention during her frequent drives through the capital city.

Two of the Wilson girls, Jessie and Eleanor, were married in the White House early in their father's Presidency — Eleanor to Wilson's Secretary of the Treasury, William G. McAdoo. Then, in August 1914, the family was stunned by the death of the First Lady, a victim of Bright's disease. Once again, a coffin was placed in the East Room; once again, grief engulfed a First Family.

The President's sorrow was genuine and deep, but within eight months he was thoroughly smitten by an attractive widow who would become his second wife and, in the opinion of many of her contemporaries, the first woman President of the United States.

Edith Bolling Galt, like Wilson, was a Virginian by birth. A descendant of Pocahontas and John Rolfe, she was the daughter of a plantation owner and the widow of a Washington jeweler who had left her his lucrative business. She was forty-two years old when she became a friend of Helen Bones, a cousin of Wilson's whom he had asked to serve as his White House hostess after Ellen's death. The two ladies went to the White House for tea after a walk one day, Mrs. Galt having been assured that the President, whom she had never met, was playing golf. Wilson returned in time to meet her, and to join them for tea. Miss Bones and Dr. Cary Grayson, Wilson's doctor and close friend, were amazed to hear the recently bereaved President laughing at Mrs. Galt's witticisms. "I can't say that I foresaw in the first minute what was going to happen,"

Helen Bones said later. "It may have taken ten minutes."

From that first meeting on, Mrs. Galt was a frequent guest at the White House. Two months later, on the South Portico, Wilson declared his love openly for the first time. His close advisers warned him that remarriage so soon after his first wife's death could cost him reelection, but he and Mrs. Galt were married in her Washington home in December 1915.

In the election of the following year, Wilson narrowly defeated Charles Evans Hughes and won a second term. But although he had campaigned on the slogan "He kept us out of war," America became an active participant in World War I a month after Wilson's second inauguration. At the White House, a flock of sheep grazed on the lawn, and ninety pounds of their wool was auctioned off for $100,000, the proceeds going to the Red Cross. A war garden was planted, and like the rest of the nation, the First Family observed meatless and wheatless days. Edith Wilson's sewing machine was kept busy turning out garments to be distributed to the wounded by the Red Cross.

It was, Wilson told the nation, the war to end wars, the war to "make the world safe for democracy." After the Armistice was declared on November 11, 1918, Wilson went to Europe himself, to participate personally in the peace conference at Versailles. There he saw many of his idealistic proposals fall prey to the victorious Allies' desire for vengeance, but he rested all his hopes on the proposed League of Nations and returned to the United States convinced that Congress would ratify the peace treaty and approve America's entrance into the League.

Partly because of his own stubbornness in refusing to consult with the Republican leaders who controlled Congress, Wilson found himself bitterly opposed on the question of the League of Nations. He therefore took his case to the people, embarking on an arduous tour during which he delivered some forty speeches in thirty cities within twenty days. Then, at Pueblo, Colorado, he became ill and was quickly brought back to Washington. On October 2, 1919, at the White House, he suffered a severe stroke, which left him paralyzed on his left side.

Thus began what became uncharitably known as "Mrs. Wilson's regency." Edith Wilson was an apolitical person with only two years of formal schooling; she had no desire to be a power behind the throne. But her husband's life was in danger and she was determined to protect him. In her memoirs, she asserts that one of Wilson's doctors spoke to her as follows:

Have everything come to you; weigh the importance of each matter, and see if it is possible by consultations with the respective heads of the Departments to solve them without the guidance of your husband. In this way you can save him a great deal. But always keep in mind that every time you take him a new anxiety or problem to excite him, you are turning a knife in an open wound.

For months, therefore, the government of the United States operated at Mrs. Wilson's discretion. Memoranda, petitions, queries to the Chief Executive were all monitored by the First Lady, who ignored most of them and dealt only with those that she regarded as crucial. A scrawl that was purportedly the President's signature appeared on some documents, but no one could be sure who had actually made it. Meandering around the margins of letters and memos were handwritten notes from the First Lady, ostensibly relaying the President's instructions. But rumors about what actually was happening on the second floor of the mansion flew around town wildly. The President was totally paralyzed; the President was insane; the President was suffering from advanced syphilis.

Wilson improved very slowly, and a few people were allowed to see him. Among them were the King and Queen of the Belgians, who were surprised by his white beard, and England's young Prince of Wales, later the Duke of Windsor. To the latter, with great effort, the partially paralyzed President was able to relate haltingly the history of the bed in which he lay; it had belonged, he told the prince, to Abraham Lincoln.

In mid-November, the President was allowed to leave his room for the first time. Seated in a rolling chair obtained from the Atlantic City, New Jersey, boardwalk, and wrapped warmly against the cold, Wilson was wheeled out onto the South Portico for some fresh air. From the Cabinet room in the executive wing, the department heads could see their stricken leader. None was allowed to visit him in his room, however. "I am not interested in the President of the United States," Edith reiterated. "I am interested in my husband and his health."

Bitterly, the Cabinet complained that their letters were ignored, their requests undelivered. Secretary of State Lansing concluded that the President was "utterly unable to attend to public business." He sent to the President, he said, "memoranda reduced to the simplest form which anyone could understand," and

received in return "answers communicated through
Mrs. Wilson so confused that no one could interpret
them."

There was, of course, talk of removing the President
from office, of impeaching him because of his inability
to perform the job. In December, two of the opposition
senators who hoped to bring about the impeachment
were finally allowed to see the President. Mrs. Wilson,
Dr. Grayson, and Joseph Tumulty, the President's secretary, carefully set the stage for the visit, and rehearsed
with the President every move he would make. Papers
were placed at his right, so that he could pick them up
with his good hand. Blankets covered his paralyzed
left arm. Of course, Wilson's ability to converse and to
hold a train of thought was questionable, but on the
occasion of the visit, the President marshaled all his
strength for one grueling effort. He was able to shake
hands firmly, wave his guests to chairs with his good
hand, and speak strongly and clearly. As the surprised
senators left, one of them said, "Mr. President, we have
all been praying for you." "Which way, senator?" asked
the President. The hastily departing senators were obliged to tell waiting reporters the truth; the President
had seemed in full control of his faculties. Talk of
impeachment subsided.

In the months that followed, White House life
evolved into a sad pattern. At eight each morning
Wilson was lifted from his bed to a chair by his valet.
The First Lady read newspaper headlines to him as he
ate breakfast. A short session of official business followed, if Wilson was up to it. The President spoke
little, often forgetting his train of thought in the
middle of a sentence.

Late each morning, he was wheeled to the East Room where a silent film was shown; a different picture was projected each day. An airing on the lawn or portico was followed by lunch, a nap, and another work session, if possible. Later, Edith read to him, usually from a mystery novel. Often, for no apparent reason, Wilson would break into tears.

The constant barrage of criticism depressed the First Lady, but somehow she persisted in her course of action. Wilson's irrational behavior did not help. When he learned that his Cabinet had been meeting without him in an effort to keep channels of communication open, he became enraged and fired the Secretary of State. When his favorite car broke down, he refused to go out in any other and would go for rides only in a horsedrawn carriage. More tragically, he refused obstinately to compromise in any way in regard to the League of Nations, and because of his intransigence, all chance of American participation in the League was lost.

In April 1920, he met with his Cabinet for the first time since the stroke. He looked, according to the Secretary of Agriculture, "old, worn and haggard; it was enough to make one weep." Meetings were held occasionally thereafter, but Wilson repeated himself, lost track of the arguments, and proved incapable of conducting fruitful sessions. In time, he began to see foreign diplomats again (the encounters were often embarrassing to the envoys) and to go for rides more often. Each evening, his valet would dress Wilson in a dinner jacket, and the President and Edith would dine together, usually in silence, in the upstairs library. Incredibly, Wilson began to harbor hopes of winning an-

other nomination from his party. But it was Governor James Cox of Ohio who was named by the Democrats that summer. Wilson's disappointment was alleviated by the dedication of Cox and his running mate, young Franklin Delano Roosevelt, to the League. In November, however, the handsome and incompetent Warren Harding was swept into office by the voters.

In March 1921 Wilson vacated the White House at last, ending one of the strangest and potentially most dangerous episodes in White House history. The former President died three years later, in the S Street house that he and Edith had purchased as his second term came to a close.

While still in the White House, the President had announced to Edith his intention of writing a book on government after his term ended. But all he ever wrote was the following dedication, typed with his good hand:

A Dedication

To E. B. W.

I dedicate this book because it is a book in which I have tried to interpret life, the life of a nation, and she has shown me the full meaning of life. Her heart is not only true but wise; her thoughts are not only free but touched with vision; she teaches and guides by being what she is; her unconscious interpretation of faith and duty makes all the way clear; her power to comprehend makes work and thoughts alike easier and more near to what it seeks.

VI
Franklin and Eleanor

"Oh *dearest* Eleanor — it is simply too nice to be true," wrote Princess Alice from the White House in November 1904; "you old fox not to tell me before." President Theodore Roosevelt was equally pleased to learn of the engagement of his niece Eleanor to young Franklin Delano Roosevelt, their distant cousin. "No other success in life — not the Presidency, or anything else — begins to compare with the joy and happiness that come in and from the love of the true man and the true woman . . ." T.R. wrote to the groom-to-be.

The President happily agreed to give away the bride, whose parents were both dead, at the wedding in New York the following March. (If she had ever heard the current witticism that the ebullient T.R. wished to be the bride at every wedding he attended and the corpse at every funeral, Eleanor did not let it interfere with her pleasure at having her famous uncle in attendance.) Two weeks before the nuptials, the handsome scion of the Hyde Park Roosevelts and his radiant fiancée traveled to Washington with the rest of the Roosevelt clan to attend T.R.'s second inauguration. To both Franklin and Eleanor, the White House was familiar ground. She had often been a guest there during her uncle's first term, and Franklin had visited the historic mansion on several occasions. "My little man," he had been told by President Cleveland when as a five-year-old he had accompanied his father to the White House, "I am making a strange wish for you. I hope that you may never be President of the United States."

Knowing that T.R. had pledged not to seek a third term, the assembled Roosevelts undoubtedly thought that they were attending the last presidential inaugura-

tion that could be regarded as a family affair. They could not have then suspected, of course, that Cleveland's wish for young Franklin would not come true, that twenty-eight years after T.R.'s inauguration Franklin and Eleanor would move into the White House themselves and live there longer than any First Family in the nation's history.

In the years between the two Roosevelts, the United States sent its sons to fight in Europe, enjoyed unprecedented prosperity, and then succumbed to the most severe economic depression in the country's experience. During those dramatic years — as always — the White House was the scene of laughter and elation, anger and frustration, and more than a normal amount of sorrow.

For Warren Harding, especially, the Presidency was an intolerable burden. The handsome senator from Ohio was elected to succeed the stricken Woodrow Wilson not because of his ability, which was modest at best, but because his good-natured pliability made him an ideal candidate from the viewpoint of the political bosses, and his good looks and inoffensiveness appealed to the voters — particularly women, who in 1920 were participating in a presidential election for the first time. At first, Harding was delighted to be President. He enjoyed playing golf on the White House grounds, welcoming his cronies to late-night poker games, and allowing his ambitious wife, Florence — known as "the Duchess" — to entertain lavishly. He soon discovered that the demands of the office were too great for him, however, and to make matters worse, he realized that his friends were busily filling their pockets at the public's expense. "In this job," the troubled President remarked as he left for a western trip in

Harding

Coolidge

Hoover

F. D. Roosevelt

1923, "I am not worried about my enemies. It is my friends that are keeping me awake nights."

Harding's death in San Francisco that August — probably from a blood clot in the brain — saved him the anguish of public disclosure of his friends' dishonesty. By the time the Teapot Dome oil lease scandal and other frauds perpetrated during the Harding administration came to light, Calvin Coolidge had inherited the Presidency.

Coolidge was evidently as parsimonious and tight-lipped as all the jokes about him suggested. His wife, Grace, on the other hand, was attractive and outgoing. She must have been good-natured and loving to put up with Coolidge's many practical jokes — he was fond, for instance, of pressing all the buzzers that called the servants, and then disappearing — and his insistence on personally supervising all the details of White House life. The First Lady bought no clothes without Coolidge's approval, and it was to him, not to Mrs. Coolidge, that menus and other housekeeping plans were submitted. The President often made unannounced tours of inspection, to make sure that everything was being done properly. On one occasion, he wandered into the kitchen before a state dinner and was upset to discover that six hams had been prepared. Even though sixty guests were expected, Coolidge thought that too much food had been purchased.

"It was my desire to maintain about the White House as far as possible an attitude of simplicity," he said later. "There is no need of theatricals." Nevertheless, Coolidge did not object to donning Indian headdresses, cowboy chaps, or other regalia for the photographers, nor to posing with White House guests, in-

cluding Queen Marie of Rumania, Will Rogers, and Charles Lindbergh, all of whom visited the mansion during his occupancy. More often than not, guests discovered that the President's nickname, Silent Cal, was all too accurate.

The great personal tragedy of Coolidge's Presidency was the death of his second son, Calvin, Jr., soon after Coolidge had been nominated for a full term of his own in 1924. Blood poisoning, the result of a seemingly unimportant blister on his heel, took the life of the sixteen-year-old boy. "I do not know why such a price was exacted for occupying the White House," wrote the sorrowing Chief Executive.

During Coolidge's administration, the White House underwent another of its periodic renovations. A survey by Army engineers had revealed that the roof beams were rotten and that a new roof was a necessity. With characteristic sarcasm, the President remarked that "there were plenty others who would be willing to take the risk" of living under that particular roof, but he and the First Lady would move out of the mansion so that the work could done.

Since the roof had to be removed anyway, it was decided to enlarge the third floor and add some badly needed new rooms. Chambers for guests and servants were constructed, along with rooms for sewing, storage, and other housekeeping purposes. A sun room, which Mrs. Coolidge referred to as "the sky-parlor," was built above the South Portico.

At Mrs. Coolidge's request, Congress passed a resolution authorizing White House occupants to accept antique or historic furniture or art that citizens might wish to donate. But the resolution resulted in few con-

tributions. Mrs. Coolidge's own gift to the mansion was a bedspread for the huge Lincoln bed; it took the First Lady two years to crochet it.

Coolidge's successor, Herbert Hoover, was swept into office in 1928 by an electorate that liked his pledge of continued Republican prosperity. Within a few months of his inauguration in March 1929, however, the stock market had collapsed and the country was gripped by the Great Depression. Hoover announced periodically that the economy was sound and that the end of the slump was in sight. Perhaps to demonstrate their confidence in the future, he and his wife entertained constantly, far more than most first families. The stream of White House guests seemed endless; sometimes three or four thousand invitations went out for a single reception. To inform the President and the Cabinet that a reception was about to end, the band was usually instructed to play "The Blue Danube Waltz." That music was selected because one Cabinet wife had informed Mrs. Hoover that it was the only song her husband could recognize other than "The Star-Spangled Banner."

Once, Mrs. Hoover gave a linen shower for a secretary who was about to be married. Recalling that Abigail Adams had hung her laundry in the East Room, she held the shower there, and all the gifts were hung on a clothesline! The First Lady's sense of history was demonstrated in a more orthodox manner when she furnished one parlor on the second floor with authentic pieces from the Monroe administration and replicas of furniture associated with the Monroes.

By far the most noteworthy redecoration of the Hoover occupancy was "the indoor retreat" that the First Lady created at one end of the second-floor hall. Journalist Bess Furman later described the new room:

> What Mrs. Hoover had done was to block off the western, or sunset, end of the great central corridor, and had it turned into a palm room of more than hotel-lobby proportions. On the floor was a green fiber rug, to add to its outdoorsy air, and the furniture was indeed of the "summer" type, an expensive and heavy bamboo. Across the entire width of the picture window was one of the world's largest cages of canaries. Other birdcages hung from the tall standards among the palms. It was an astonishing bit of interior decoration for antique-minded Washington, but well done, cool-looking, and restful.

Another room that Hoover prized was the small chamber off the President's bedroom. There he displayed all the drawings and paintings of himself that had been sent to the White House by amateur artists. Needless to say, the degree of artistic success varied considerably. Hoover enjoyed bringing guests to the room and laughing with them over the many attempts to capture his likeness.

Laughter became increasingly rare in the White House, however. The economic depression deepened and the suffering grew ever more widespread. Hoover believed that state and local governments were responsible for alleviating the situation, that Washington had only limited power. His inflexibility was no help, nor was his refusal to talk with representatives of such malcontent groups as the bonus marchers of 1932. The episode of the Bonus Army, in fact, marks the nadir of the Hoover Presidency. Several thousand unemployed World War I veterans, who had been promised that

In 1923 a President's coffin again lay in state in the East Room (left, above). Warren Harding had died a few months before disclosures of corruption disgraced his administration. Harding's successor, Calvin Coolidge, posing above with a party of Sioux chiefs, did not look much like a President, being pale and thin and "apparently deficient in red corpuscles," as a neighbor once wrote. But he restored dignity to the office, and added a bit of wry humor. Grace Coolidge, a popular and hospitable First Lady, appears with her white collie in Howard Chandler Christy's beautiful portrait (left), which now hangs in the White House in the China Room.

Elected by a landslide in 1928, Herbert Hoover, shown at left in his favorite cartoon portrait, quickly lost popularity when his policies failed to ease the deepening economic crisis. Hoover refused to authorize public relief measures, and when World War I veterans marched on Washington in 1932 demanding early bonus payments, the President ordered the Army to move them out. At right, marchers struggle with capital police, while at far right, wearing riding boots and jodhpurs, General Douglas MacArthur and Major Dwight Eisenhower oversee the dispersal of the demonstrators.

they would receive a bonus in 1945, marched on Washington to demand immediate payment. Camping along the Anacostia River in huts and shacks, many of them refused to leave the city even after Congress had rejected their request. Hoover ordered the Army to evict them, and troops under the command of General Douglas MacArthur and Major Dwight D. Eisenhower used tanks and tear gas to scatter the squatters and then set fire to their shantytown. The sky over Washington was red from the flames, clearly visible from the windows of the nearby White House.

It was Franklin Delano Roosevelt who restored faith in the government and confidence in the nation's future, who took charge firmly and convinced the American people — as he announced in his stirring inaugural address on March 4, 1933 — that "the only thing we have to fear is fear itself." Not since Theodore Roosevelt had a man of such self-assurance and charisma occupied the White House. Espousing no single formula, he was willing to try anything that might alleviate the suffering and put the country on the road to recovery.

Stricken with polio at the age of thirty-nine, President Roosevelt was paralyzed from the hips down. To stand, he needed steel braces that locked at the knees. A cane and the strong arm of a son or friend were required when he walked; usually he used a wheelchair to move about. Yet most Americans never thought of F.D.R. as an invalid. His handsome face, irresistible smile, and hearty laugh quickly dispelled any inclination to think of him as a sick man, and the strong, resonant voice that spoke to the nation so often over the radio exuded confidence and optimism.

F.D.R. was loathed by some Americans. To them he was "that man in the White House," a traitor to his class and to his country. But to a vast majority of the citizens he was an increasingly beloved leader, one who earned their total trust and held their continuing allegiance. It was he who led them out of the Great Depression, and it was to him that they granted unprecedented third and fourth terms in 1940 and 1944, so that he might lead them through another ordeal, World War II.

As for Eleanor, there never had been, nor is there ever likely to be, another First Lady like her. Although she always denied that she could influence her husband, she played a key role in making the Roosevelt administration responsive to the needs and rights of the underprivileged and of minority groups. Negroes and Jews, the young and the elderly, the poor and the homeless, women of all classes — all came to regard the White House as a symbol not of despair and impotence but of hope and action.

Mrs. Roosevelt made it clear right from the beginning that she intended to do things her own way, regardless of tradition. She shocked the White House staff several weeks before F.D.R.'s inauguration by arriving on foot for an inspection visit; offers of an official limousine had been repeatedly refused by the strong-willed Eleanor, who insisted on walking from her hotel to the mansion. Ike Hoover, the chief usher and no relation to the departing First Family, later reported that she gave him instructions that day with remarkable dispatch:

[She] rattled it off as if she had known it her whole life. She had already decided on every last detail of

the social plans for Inauguration Day; told me who the house guests would be and what rooms they would occupy, though this was five weeks in the future; gave me the menus for the meals, both regular and special; told me what household effects she would bring; what servants should be provided for; what the family liked for meals and when they liked to have them; in fact everything the Chief Usher could wish to know except what the weather might be on March fourth.

The new First Lady loved the White House. In a way, it was more of a home to her than the family estate in Hyde Park or the Roosevelt house in New York City, both of which were really the domains of the President's domineering mother, Sara Delano Roosevelt, who exerted far too much influence over the affairs of her son's family. In the White House, however, Eleanor was very much the mistress. "I think it is a beautiful house," she wrote once, "with lovely proportions, great dignity, and I do not think anyone looking at it from the outside or living in it can fail to feel the spell of the past and the responsibility of living up to the fine things which have been done and lived in that house." Having visited there so often in the past, Eleanor was in no way intimidated by the mansion; she was not afraid to turn it into a home that would be comfortable for her husband, her children, and her grandchildren.

"You know how it was when Uncle Ted was here," F.D.R. had said of the mansion right after his election, "how gay and homelike. Well, that's how we mean to have it." When the Roosevelt boys complained that the refrigerators were locked at night, Eleanor made sure that midnight snacks were always available. She had play equipment installed on the roof for the grand-

children, and a sandbox and jungle gym were erected for them on the lawn. Told by an official that old-fashioned swings could not be hung from the trees for fear of injuring historic bark, Eleanor simply bided her time until the moment was right, and then had a swing put up.

To the dismay of the staff, Eleanor insisted on operating the elevator herself, and if the furniture seemed to need rearranging, she saw nothing wrong with a First Lady shoving a chair or two around. Always solicitous of others, she realized that the servants' facilities were inadequate and had the kitchen and staff dressing and dining rooms enlarged. During that renovation, a cow trough that had been used during the Jackson administration was uncovered by workmen. The contractor took it away, but when F.D.R. heard about the discovery, he demanded the return of the trough, which was subsequently placed on the south lawn and filled with flowers.

Removing the fragile Monroe furniture from the second-floor parlor, Eleanor installed "good substantial furniture and never worried about breakage." Mrs. Hoover's "greenhouse effects" at the end of the corridor were quickly removed and also replaced with more durable and comfortable furniture. Mrs. Roosevelt usually had her breakfast there, and she also served tea there each afternoon, using a silver tea service that had been a wedding present from Alice Roosevelt.

The second-floor Oval Room was set aside as the President's study. His collection of naval prints adorned the walls, and when an Ethiopian prince gave him a lion's skin, it was placed on the floor there and became one of the President's favorite possessions. Each

"MOTHER, WILFRED WROTE A BAD WORD!"

Grinning broadly, his trademark cigarette holder jutting at a rakish angle from between his teeth, Franklin D. Roosevelt conveyed an image of confidence that did almost as much to relieve the depression as his multitude of New Deal programs. Reelected in 1936 by the greatest margin in American history, the President also inspired deep hostility. In some homes his name was almost an obscenity — as reflected in the 1938 cartoon at right.

evening F.D.R. served cocktails before dinner to his staff and to whichever of his children happened to be at home at the time; Eleanor, who did not enjoy liquor, usually eschewed the cocktail hour, which was a time for "the Boss" and his intimates to exchange jokes and laugh over the day's events.

Among the permanent residents of the mansion were Marguerite LeHand, F.D.R.'s secretary, who was assigned a suite on the third floor so that she would always be near at hand if the President needed her, and Louis Howe, Roosevelt's political mentor and most trusted aide. When Howe died in 1936, he was afforded the honor of an East Room funeral. Later in the Roosevelt Presidency, Harry Hopkins became F.D.R.'s closest confidant and he too moved into the White House.

"I was interested," Eleanor once said about F.D.R.'s first day in office, "because I felt that with my husband's sense of history the first night in the White House would be a tremendously historic, impressive thing to him. But on this occasion, to my surprise, he behaved exactly as though he had always been there, and never anywhere else. He worked immediately on his first problem, which was the problem of closing the banks."

Fast, firm action was the keynote of Roosevelt's New Deal. Proposals for legislation and executive orders emerged from the White House with assembly-line speed and precision. The old mansion was alive with activity, as F.D.R. and his Brain Trust broke all the molds and came up with innovation after innovation to stop the depression. The President's frequent "fireside chats" to the nation assured him of the people's support, and he won the admiration of the press corps by announcing that questions to be asked at his press

conferences need not be submitted in advance, although reporters could not directly quote his replies. Eleanor, too, held a weekly press conference, and she thus made the White House a prime news source for the ladies of the press.

The First Lady also wrote a newspaper column of her own — "My Day" — and had a regular radio program. She was ubiquitous — going everywhere and doing everything, from serving food at a soup kitchen to reading to children in the hard-hit Dust Bowl. F.D.R. often asked her to travel for political purposes, but usually she went because she wanted to, because she saw some way in which her presence could help the downtrodden. Always, she called to F.D.R.'s attention any unfair situation and urged him to correct injustice even if the move were politically unwise.

It was Eleanor who saw to it that no group was excluded from the mansion. No one was surprised, for example, when she entertained a group of sharecroppers in the Red Room. Mrs. Roosevelt was well aware of the value of the White House as an opinion-making weapon. In 1936 she gave a garden party for the staff and inmates of the capital city's Training School for Delinquent Girls. The First Lady had visited the institution and been appalled at conditions there. She knew that by inviting the girls — a majority of whom were black — to the White House, she would create a furor in some quarters. But she also knew that the attention of Congress would be focused on the problem as in no other way. The First Lady was indeed attacked by racists and by many newspapers — just as she had been when she invited Marian Anderson to sing at the White House, and just as her Uncle Theodore had been after

'BUT IT WOULD MAKE SUCH A NICE SCOOP IF YOU'D ONLY TELL ME, FRANKLIN.'

he had asked Booker T. Washington to stay for dinner. But criticism of that sort never bothered the First Lady, who acted as she thought was right.

Whenever she could, Mrs. Roosevelt tried to set an example that would profit all American women. When, for instance, a nutrition expert devised a set of menus that were cheap as well as nourishing, the First Lady felt compelled to serve them at the White House. Thus F.D.R. was treated to a "7-cent luncheon," consisting of hot stuffed eggs with tomato sauce, mashed potatoes, prune pudding, bread, and coffee. The menu was well publicized, but the President was not pleased. Eleanor, for her part, cared nothing for food, and she found it hard to understand why F.D.R. complained so often about the White House cooking. Lillian Parks, who worked as a maid at the mansion, recalled that "Mr. Roosevelt complained to her [Eleanor] once that he had been given chicken six times in one week. She said: 'Impossible, Franklin.' But they checked back on the menus, and it was true. Another time he told her he was so hungry he had to eat two ambassadors!"

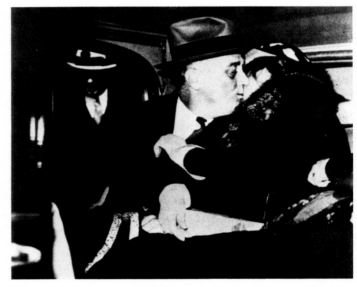

Despite her travels and the innumerable demands on her time, Mrs. Roosevelt was an active hostess. Everyone came to the White House: movie stars and kings, politicians and scientists, rich and poor. During one year — 1939 — the following figures were compiled: 4,729 people came to a meal at the White House; 323 people were houseguests there; 9,311 people came to tea; 14,056 people were entertained at receptions. The large receptions were arduous, but as Mrs. Roosevelt later wrote:

I think to many people the White House, in itself, symbolizes the government, and though standing and

LINCOLN DIDN'T
WASHINGTON WOULDN'T
ROOSEVELT SHOULDN'T

WE DON'T WANT ELEANOR EITHER

shaking hands for an hour or so, two or three times a week, is not exactly an inspiring occupation, still I think it well worth while. I did it regularly, three times a week, during the winter months.

Mrs. Roosevelt's supply of energy seemed limitless. She rarely complained of fatigue, although she once did admit that "so many people have been in and out of the house the last few days, and so many more will be these next few days, that I ache at the thought. I'm always thankful for these hours from 1:00 to 3:00." She meant, of course, one to three in the morning, which was often the only time she had to catch up with her personal correspondence.

F.D.R. too seemed to thrive on the pressures and ceaseless activity of the Presidency. He relaxed by swimming daily in the new White House pool, paid for by public contributions; by working on his famous stamp collection; and by watching the Hollywood movies that were shown two or three times a week at the mansion — always with a Mickey Mouse cartoon if one was available.

Reelected by an unprecedented landslide in 1936, F.D.R. found more and more of his time occupied by foreign affairs. The aggression of Germany, Italy, and Japan was rapidly bringing the world to the brink of war, and Roosevelt saw what lay ahead all too clearly. As early as 1937, he warned the American people that an "epidemic of world lawlessness" was spreading. "Innocent people, innocent nations are being cruelly sacrificed to a greed for power. . . . If those things come to pass in other parts of the world, let no one imagine that America will escape." By 1940, when F.D.R. made his controversial decision to seek a third term, Hitler con-

trolled continental Europe and Nazi bombs were falling on England; Japan, having swept across much of Asia, was invading French Indochina. F.D.R. told the voters that fall that he hoped to keep America out of the war but asked support for a program of national defense that would make the United States what he would later call the "arsenal of democracy." In an unparalleled display of faith in a leader, the American people reelected Roosevelt.

On December 7, 1941, Eleanor Roosevelt entertained a large group of guests for lunch, but the President remained in his study with Harry Hopkins. There they learned of the Japanese attack on Pearl Harbor. Later in that hectic day, Eleanor went in to see him:

When I did go in I thought he was looking very tired and strained. But he was completely calm. It was always like that when things were really bad: he became just like an iceberg, and there was this deadly calm. . . . He reacted in the same way he did during the banking crisis. He started at once to do the things he had to do — and with a perfect assurance the country would be able to meet any situation whatever.

Consulting with his military aides, F.D.R. looked out across the White House lawn and recalled a similarly critical moment in American history. "From this same window," he said, "Lincoln watched the Confederate campfires twinkling across the Potomac."

In wartime as in peace, F.D.R. was able to communicate to the nation his strength and confidence. On Christmas Eve, only seventeen days after Pearl Harbor, a large crowd gathered at the White House, where for one night the blackout was suspended and floodlights illuminated the mansion. Accompanied by Winston

In Douglas Chandor's multiple portrait (left), Eleanor Roosevelt's expressive hands emphasize her vitality and spontaneity. Painted in 1949 and now on view in the ground-floor corridor of the White House, the portrait is the only one for which Mrs. Roosevelt formally posed. In the upper right-hand corner is her inscription: "A trial made pleasant by the painter—Eleanor Roosevelt." In the 1939 photograph shown at right, the First Lady rides in a Washington procession with visiting Queen Elizabeth of England.

Churchill, who had come to Washington for consultations, F.D.R. threw a switch that turned on the lights of an enormous Christmas tree. It was an effective symbol of Roosevelt's faith that the aggressors would be crushed.

Once again, the White House became the headquarters of a great military effort. For the first time in history, however, aerial attack on the Executive Mansion became a possibility. Gun crews were stationed on the roof, and gas masks were distributed to the residents; one mask was kept fastened to F.D.R.'s wheelchair at all times. Blackout curtains were hung on the windows, and periodic air-raid drills were held. Public tours of the mansion were cancelled, the military guard outside was increased, and an underground shelter was constructed. Although connected to the White House, the shelter was actually in the basement of the nearby Treasury Department. "Henry," F.D.R. told Secretary of the Treasury Morgenthau, "I will not go down in the shelter unless you allow me to play poker with all the gold in your vaults."

In a room on the ground floor that had been devoted to the display of various trophies, a map room was established for the President. As he followed troop movements and studied battle reports there, F.D.R. must often have thought of his own four sons, all of whom were in the military service.

During the war, there was an almost constant procession of distinguished visitors to the White House. The Queen of Holland, the King of Greece, the other monarchs whose countries had succumbed to the Nazi blitzkrieg came to see F.D.R., as did the ministers and rulers of many other allied nations. The White House

staff took most of these distinguished visitors in stride, having already taken care of the King and Queen of England, during their visit to the White House in June 1939.

That gracious and undemanding royal couple were liked by everyone, although some members of their entourage seemed overly conscious of their own importance and demanded constant attention. The staff at the mansion was particularly amused when the English party asked for hot-water bottles and extra blankets at night, even though Washington was undergoing a summer heat wave. To entertain the king and queen, Eleanor arranged an evening of native American music. Kate Smith sang "When the Moon Comes Over the Mountain"—a special request of the king—and Marian Anderson sang Negro spirituals. Ballad singers and dancers from the South performed American folk songs. After the official White House entertainment, the royal couple went to Hyde Park with the Roosevelts, who arranged for them to attend a typical American picnic, replete with hot dogs.

After war broke out in 1941, Churchill was a frequent guest at the White House. The former Monroe Room on the second floor became his personal map room. He and the President would confer late into the night, discussing the war and the future peace. Churchill napped each afternoon, so he remained fresh, but it took F.D.R. some time to catch up on his sleep after each of Churchill's visits. Eleanor found Churchill "very human & I like him tho' I don't want him to control the peace." He and F.D.R. worked well together, however, and enjoyed a warm rapport. Once, during a Churchill visit, the two leaders tried to think

of a name for the world organization that the President had proposed. Later that night, an enthusiastic F.D.R. rolled his wheelchair into the room in which Churchill was bathing to tell him that he had thought of a name: the United Nations. A pink and soggy Churchill shared the President's excitement.

According to William C. Mott, a Navy officer who was assigned to the White House, "Mr. Churchill loved our map room and he was likely to come there at any hour of the day or night. His visits were most often announced by a little round fat face peering around the corner and asking, 'How's Hitler? The ba-astard.'"

Another guest at the Executive Mansion was V. M. Molotov of Russia, whose visit was not publicized and who was officially listed as "Mr. Brown." The White House servant who unpacked his bag was astonished to find a hunk of black bread, a roll of sausage, and a pistol.

Madame Chiang Kai-shek, wife of the Chinese president, stayed at the mansion several times. Fragile and lovely, she was liked by the Roosevelts but not by the staff, who found her and her entourage far too imperious. They clapped their hands royally every time they needed assistance ("They think they're in China calling the coolies," commented one servant), and Madame Chiang demanded that the silk sheets she carried with her be ironed freshly after each use. Since she was given to frequent, brief naps, the sheets had to be removed, ironed, and replaced often.

In later years, Mrs. Roosevelt recalled a moment with Madame Chiang that amused the President:

I had painted for Franklin such a sweet, gentle and pathetic figure that, as he came to recognize the other

side of the lady, it gave him keen pleasure to tease me about my lack of perception. I remember an incident at a dinner party during one of her visits which gave him particular entertainment. John Lewis was acting up at the time, and Franklin turned to Madame Chiang and asked, "What would you do in China with a labor leader like John Lewis?" She never said a word, but the beautiful, small hand came up very quietly and slid across her throat — a most expressive gesture. Franklin looked across at me to make sure I had seen, and went right on talking. He knew that I would understand and make allowances for the differences in background and customs; nevertheless he enjoyed being able to say to me afterwards: "Well, how about your gentle and sweet character?"

Eleanor continued to travel widely throughout the war years. She visited England, South America, the South Pacific, and remained as indefatigable as ever. The President, however, began to show all too clearly the toll taken by years of economic and military crisis. His fourth inauguration, in January 1945, was a happy occasion, attended by all thirteen of his grandchildren. But everyone who looked at F.D.R. could tell that he was an exhausted and weakened man. Following the swearing-in, which took place on the South Portico of the White House rather than at the Capitol, the President had collapsed in his eldest son's arms. "I knew that his days were numbered," James Roosevelt said later.

Two days after the inauguration, the President flew to Yalta for his final diplomatic conference with Stalin and Churchill. He "seemed placid and frail," Churchill recalled. "I felt that he had a slender contact with life." Addressing Congress upon his return, F.D.R. re-

Weakened by the strain of twelve years in the White House and by his arduous campaign for a fourth term, a haggard and drawn Roosevelt sits with Winston Churchill and Joseph Stalin in the photo at left, taken at Yalta during the last of the Big Three conferences in February 1945. (F.D.R. always sat between the other two, who could scarcely tolerate each other.) Standing are Anthony Eden, Edward Stettinius (F.D.R.'s Secretary of State), Vyacheslav Molotov, and W. Averell Harriman. Returning to Washington even weaker than before, F.D.R. — the only President many young people had ever known — died two months later. Below, his funeral cortege moves through the capital.

mained seated, pleading exhaustion and making reference to his paralysis — the first time he had ever done so in public.

The war was all but won that spring, when Roosevelt journeyed to Warm Springs, Georgia, where he often went for rest and physical therapy. But on April 12, 1945, a massive cerebral hemorrhage took his life.

It was at the White House that the First Lady learned of her husband's death, and it was there that, controlling her own personal grief, she later told the awful news to Vice President Harry S. Truman. As always, Eleanor Roosevelt thought not of herself but of others. When a stunned Truman asked her what he could do for her, she replied, "Is there anything *we* can do for *you*? For you are the one in trouble now."

VII
Renovation and Restoration

"Found the White House 'falling down,'" President Harry S. Truman wrote one day in August 1948. "My daughter's sitting room floor had broken down into the family dining room. . . . The White House architect and engineer have moved me into the southeast or Lincoln Room — for safety — imagine that!"

Truman had been living in the White House for more than three years, so he was well aware that the old mansion was not in the best of condition. The floor of his oval study on the second story swayed and creaked as he walked across it. The chandelier in the Blue Room was given to swinging back and forth ominously, and there were innumerable other signs that the house was structurally weak. When a leg of Margaret Truman's grand piano (which had been hoisted through a window when the family moved in, in May 1945) broke through the ceiling of the room below, it was clear that immediate action was necessary.

The architects and engineers who examined the White House over the ensuing weeks were appalled at its condition. The enlargement of the third floor in 1927 had critically overburdened the structure. The old walls and beams had been cut into so often, to accommodate various remodelings and the installation of modern pipes and wires, that the entire house was about to collapse; the family quarters on the second floor were, as the commissioner of public buildings pointed out, supported "purely by habit." A week before Truman's surprising reelection in November, it was discovered that the East Room ceiling was sagging dangerously; it was propped up by a temporary scaffold while the future of the Executive Mansion was debated.

Three courses of action were proposed and considered. One plan suggested that the White House be designated a museum, and a new residence for the President be built elsewhere. A second plan called for the razing of the mansion and the erection of a replica on the same site. Fortunately, however, sentiment and tradition carried the day. Congress adopted a third scheme, which called for the preservation of the mansion's exterior walls. The interior would be totally gutted and rebuilt, however; everything that could be saved would be dismantled, removed, and then replaced in the rebuilt mansion — which would be, in almost every respect, a replica of the original interior.

For four years, the feisty Truman and his family lived across Pennsylvania Avenue in Blair House, which had been built in 1842 for the first surgeon general of the Army, Dr. Joseph Lovell, and had later been owned by the Blair family. The President supervised the work on the Executive Mansion as it progressed. Mantelpieces, wall paneling, fixtures, decorative moldings, and friezes — all were taken apart and the pieces numbered and stored away for later reinstallation. Then the whole interior was demolished. Two subterranean basement floors were excavated and steel beams were erected to support the new interior. The entire structure was fireproofed and air-conditioned. And the historic outer walls were shored up on new foundations.

It took four years and more than $5,000,000 to rebuild the White House. But when Truman moved back in, in 1952, the presidential mansion was, as Abigail Adams had said too optimistically 150 years earlier, "built for ages to come."

Truman   *Eisenhower*

Kennedy   *L. B. Johnson*   *Nixon*

Truman had hoped to furnish the mansion with good antiques and furniture associated with past presidents. Congress vetoed the scheme as too expensive, however, and the White House was again furnished with copies of antiques and with the pieces that had been installed there during Theodore Roosevelt's 1902 renovation.

Truman lived in the White House for less than half his Presidency, yet his mark on its history is indelible. He and his family moved in on the night before V-E Day ("I am sixty-one this morning," he wrote to his mother and sister the next day, "and I slept in the President's Room in the White House last night."), and it was there that he made the momentous decision to drop atomic bombs on Japan. It was during his Presidency that World War II ended, giving way all too quickly to the tensions of cold war. Truman was the first nuclear age President; thereafter all occupants of the White House would have the awesome power to obliterate much if not all of humanity, and the equally awesome responsibility to avoid nuclear holocaust.

The outspoken Missourian took the burdens of the office in stride, however. "I had no trouble sleeping," he wrote later. "I read myself to sleep every night in the White House, reading biography or the troubles of some President in the past."

The President's cocky self-confidence made him the newspapermen's delight. His prebreakfast walks, during which reporters found it difficult to keep up with Truman's brisk pace, always resulted in a good printable quote or two and several unprintable ones. When a critic wrote unkind words about his daughter Margaret's singing, Truman wrote him a note threaten-ing to punch him in the nose. On his White House desk, he kept a copy of a Mark Twain quotation: "Always do right. This will gratify some people, and astonish the rest." It was, Truman thought, "a good sentiment."

One of Truman's most controversial acts was the erection of a balcony at the second-floor level of the White House's South Portico. The huge pillars there rose too high without relief, he felt, and the balcony would therefore be an aesthetic improvement. The floor of the balcony, he pointed out, would also provide shade for the Blue Room below and eliminate the need for unsightly awnings. And since a cool breeze from the south would reach the balcony during summer months, the residents of the mansion would have some relief from Washington's oppressive heat. Truman spent $10,000 to build his balcony, which was roundly attacked by his critics and unmercifully mocked by the nation's comedians. As always, however, the President stood firm. Later occupants of the White House have been glad that he did. The Lyndon Johnsons, for instance, dined on the balcony frequently and relaxed there often. "On a summer evening," Lady Bird Johnson was to write, Truman's balcony was "the most attractive place in the White House."

Despite the brickbats, Truman seemed to enjoy being President. His family was less enthusiastic. His wife, Bess, whom he jokingly referred to as "the Boss," was an unpretentious woman who did only what was absolutely necessary as First Lady and otherwise led as private a life as possible. In sharp contrast to her predecessor, Eleanor Roosevelt, Bess Truman did not hold press conferences or give interviews, nor did she lend

The 1948–52 renovation: above, the Truman balcony; below, the view down into the Blue Room; right, cellar excavation; far right, restoration of the Blue Room (top), and of the chandeliers (center) and floors (bottom) of the State Dining Room.

At his second inaugural in 1957, a beaming Eisenhower, with his grandchildren, stands beside the Vice President and his daughters in the photograph at left. (David Eisenhower and Julie Nixon, married in 1968, met here as shy eight-year-olds.) Ike, who was an ardent fisherman and golfer, practiced his swing on the White House lawn (right, below). He also enjoyed relaxing with a paintbrush. One of the canvases he painted during his administration, "Deserted Farm," is reproduced on the opposite page.

her support to any cause or group. Quiet evenings with relatives or old friends — with cards or movies as entertainment — were far more appealing to her than state functions. Margaret Truman, who was twenty-one years old when her father became Chief Executive, wanted only to pursue her singing career and date young men without excessive publicity; neither was possible for the President's daughter, whose omnipresent Secret Service escort was far from conducive to budding romance.

Truman's aged mother was no more at home in the White House than her daughter-in-law and granddaughter. She was ninety-two when she visited her son in the mansion, and she categorically refused to sleep in the room containing the bed associated with Lincoln. It was, she seemed to think, too awesome an honor for any mortal. "You tell Harry," she had warned, "if he puts me in the room with Lincoln's bed in it I'll sleep on the floor." She was given the Rose Guest Room instead, the room in which visiting queens stay, but that seemed far too elegant for Mrs. Truman. She slept instead in a small sitting room adjoining the Queens' Bedroom.

Dwight and Mamie Eisenhower, who succeeded the Trumans in the White House in January 1953, cherished their privacy as much as their predecessors had. They entertained when necessary but much preferred quiet evenings alone or with close friends. Their favorite room was the solarium on the third floor (Mrs. Coolidge's "sky-parlor"); there the President enjoyed cooking steaks on a portable grill, playing bridge, or watching television. During their long marriage, the Eisenhowers had moved from place to place every few

years; their eight years in the White House were their longest stay in any one home. "At last I've got a job where I can stay home nights, and, by golly, I'm going to stay home," the five-star general said.

One room on the mansion's second floor was turned into an art studio for Eisenhower, who found painting a relaxing diversion. The President also had a putting green constructed on the lawn, so that he could improve his golf game whenever he had a few free minutes.

The Eisenhowers' four grandchildren were frequent visitors, and saw to it that things never got too dull around the mansion. Aides grew accustomed to seeing tricycles in the ground-floor corridor, and a room on the third floor was turned into a playroom for the youngsters. One of the grandchildren, Mary Jean, was christened in the Blue Room. David Eisenhower, the President's grandson and the future husband of Julie Nixon, was only twelve when Eisenhower's second term ended; unhappy that his grandfather had to vacate the mansion, he wrote "I will return — Dwight David Eisenhower" on several scraps of paper and hid them under rugs and behind various paintings.

Perhaps because they knew how much their own grandchildren enjoyed playing at the White House, the Eisenhowers restored the custom of the annual Easter egg-rolling contest, to which the public was welcomed. Instituted during the administration of Rutherford B. Hayes, the event had not been held since the beginning of World War II.

During the Eisenhower Presidency, helicopters landed on the White House lawn for the first time and became a frequently used mode of presidential

transportation. Eisenhower was also the first President to permit televised White House press conferences. Actor Robert Montgomery served as a special aide to the President, coaching him so that his speeches would be effectively delivered to the millions of Americans who watched them on television. During the three serious illnesses that struck Eisenhower while he was President, his condition was reported to television audiences with a clinical thoroughness that shocked many observers. In the late nineteenth century, President Cleveland had undergone a secret shipboard operation for the removal of part of his jaw due to a malignancy, and the nation had not even suspected that anything was wrong. Modern communications, however, made presidential privacy impossible, especially in moments of grave illness.

Historians may denigrate Eisenhower's accomplishments as President, but his status as one of the most popular chief executives is unassailable; to most Americans, the Eisenhowers were beloved and admired parent, or grandparent, figures. When he left the White House in January 1961, Eisenhower had just turned seventy; he was the oldest man ever to serve as Chief Executive.

John and Jacqueline Kennedy, on the other hand, projected a very different image. Not since Theodore Roosevelt had the United States had a young and vigorous President, and not since Frances Cleveland had there been a First Lady of such youth and beauty. During the tragically brief Kennedy tenure, the White House reflected their elegance and their zest for living; in addition to its historic connotations, the mansion became the symbol of American cultural accomplish-

ment and of the nation's highest intellectual and artistic aspirations.

Much was written about "the Kennedy style," a unique blend of sophistication, intelligence, good taste, and the desire to have a good time. Women all over the country dressed as Jacqueline did, and apparently never tired of reading about her activities in magazines and newspapers; her picture on a magazine cover sold more copies than a photograph of any movie star.

During the Kennedy years, the White House was unquestionably the most glamorous and most talked about house in the nation, and invitations to functions there were more desirable than they had ever been. The Kennedys did everything possible to see that their guests enjoyed themselves. Long receiving lines were eliminated whenever possible, and mixed drinks were served, a Kennedy innovation. The menu at state dinners was shortened to four courses, and small, intimate tables were used instead of a single large one. The world's greatest artists (such as Pablo Casals, who had not played at the White House since Theodore Roosevelt's time) were asked to perform in the East Room after dinner, and after the entertainment there was dancing, which sometimes lasted until three or four in the morning. Dinners such as one honoring America's Nobel Prize winners called the nation's attention to its cultural and intellectual achievements, but everyone had a good time too.

Watching the handsome and confident President at White House parties, it was hard for guests to believe that much of the time he suffered from severe back pain, the result of an injury incurred during World War II. The rocking chair in his office, recommended

by his doctor, was well publicized; less well known was the fact that he usually wore a cloth brace, that he took daily swims in the heated pool that had been installed during F.D.R.'s administration, and that after lunch each day Kennedy napped while lying on a heating pad to alleviate the pain.

Even picking up his children was an effort for Kennedy, though that seldom stopped him from doing it. Often he would open the French doors in his Oval Office in the West Wing, walk out on the patio, and clap his hands to catch the attention of Caroline and John, Jr., playing on the south lawn — and the two would come running for a few moments of fun with their father. The antics of the children made good copy for the White House newsmen, whose readers loved to know about Caroline parading in her mother's high-heeled shoes or John-John hiding under the President's desk. The adventures of Macaroni the pony and Pushinka, the dog given Caroline by Nikita Khrushchev, were also related. Once, when asked what her father was doing, Caroline told a newsman: "Oh, he's upstairs with his shoes and socks off, not doing anything." Mrs. Kennedy established a nursery school on the third floor of the White House so that Caroline could have daily contact with other children her age.

When the First Lady lost an infant son, Patrick, two days after his birth in 1963, the nation grieved with her and the President; the boy was the first child born to an incumbent First Family since the Clevelands.

Jacqueline Kennedy's lifetime interest in art and antiques found a natural outlet in the White House. She thought it disgraceful that mediocre reproductions and pieces of no historic significance should be pre-

Using the famous rocker, prescribed by his doctor, President Kennedy meets with the ambassador from Ghana in the photograph at left. Though Kennedy was plagued by an old back injury and often in pain, his administration was one of the liveliest in decades. At the White House the First Family played host to an endless stream of glittering personalities, including many distinguished artists. At right, Mrs. Kennedy, Governor Luis Muñoz Marin of Puerto Rico, and the President (head bowed) talk with cellist Pablo Casals after his concert in the East Room. Alice Roosevelt Longworth, who was in the audience, recalled that Casals had first played at the White House in 1904, during her father's Presidency.

dominant in the nation's most famous residence. The Red Room, for instance, was furnished with Louis XV reproductions; not only was the furniture devoid of artistic merit, it was in the style of a time that antedated the establishment of the United States!

With the assistance of a newly formed Fine Arts Commission for the White House, Mrs. Kennedy sought for the mansion the finest examples of American workmanship and art, as well as items associated with the White House's former occupants. Because there were no public funds available, private gifts and donations had to be relied upon. Many superb pieces, ranging from Thomas Jefferson's inkstand to chairs originally purchased by James Monroe and a sofa of the Dolley Madison era, were presented to Mrs. Kennedy for the White House collection. A White House guidebook was compiled and sold to visitors, bringing in some $50,000 annually for new purchases.

"Everything in the White House must have a reason for being there," Mrs. Kennedy said. "It would be sacrilege merely to 'redecorate' it — a word I hate. It must be restored — and that has nothing to do with decoration. That is a question of scholarship."

In a White House basement, Mrs. Kennedy and her colleagues discovered the carved desk made from the oak timbers of the ship *Resolute* and presented to President Hayes by Queen Victoria. Installed in President Kennedy's office, it furthered the nautical motif established there by his scrimshaw collection, naval prints, and ship models. Busts of Washington and Jackson were found in a ground-floor men's room, and a pier table from the Monroe era was uncovered in the mansion's carpentry shop. In the White House storage

sheds in Virginia, Mrs. Kennedy found several chairs that had belonged to President Hayes.

In 1962, Mrs. Kennedy conducted a televised tour of the mansion, during which she proudly pointed out the results of her labors. Among her favorite acquisitions was the antique wallpaper, showing such American scenes as Niagara Falls and West Point, that had been installed in the Diplomatic Reception Room on the ground floor. A boiler room until the Theodore Roosevelt renovation of 1902, the Diplomatic Reception Room is now the first room entered by guests who arrive at the White House for state dinners. The wallpaper, printed in France in 1834 and removed from an old house in Maryland prior to its installation at the White House, serves as a superb backdrop for the Early American furniture that had been placed in the room by the Eisenhowers.

The Green Room, Mrs. Kennedy told her television audience, had been redone as a parlor of the Federal period, with furnishings dating from 1800 to 1810. Moss-green watered silk hung on the walls, and among the furniture were a sofa that had been Daniel Webster's, Martha Washington armchairs, and a beautiful mahogany secretary of the classical period that bears the label of noted Annapolis cabinetmaker John Shaw. The adjacent Red Room, hung with cerise silk with gold borders, was furnished with French and American furniture in the Empire style, all of which had been made between 1810 and 1830. The Blue Room, the formal reception room, featured decor and furnishings in the style of those used by President Monroe in 1817.

When Mrs. Kennedy conducted her tour, the Treaty Room on the second floor was still in the process of

Searching White House records and storerooms
for authentic period pieces, Jacqueline Kennedy
(shown in Aaron Shikler's 1970 portrait above)
restored the mansion's public rooms in a
manner that reflected the history of the families
that had lived there. The Victorian furnishings
of the Treaty Room (left, above), once President
Andrew Johnson's Cabinet room, include
President Grant's Cabinet table and a crystal
chandelier purchased by Grant for the East
Room. The Diplomatic Reception Room (at
left) is hung with wallpaper printed in France
in 1834, which shows views of "Scenic America";
it was transferred to the White House from an
old house in Maryland. Mrs. Kennedy was
especially proud of the Red Room, which she
furnished in the Empire style of 1810–1830, with
a sofa that once belonged to Dolley Madison.
The room, shown at right as it appeared after
Patricia Nixon's redecorating of 1972, is lit by a
gilt wooden chandelier. The walls are covered
with a specially woven silk in sumptuous cerise.

being restored. When completed, it became one of her proudest accomplishments. Originally used as a bedroom, the room had later been a reception room and a sitting room until Andrew Johnson made it his Cabinet room in 1866. The protocol to the treaty ending the war with Spain was signed there by McKinley in 1898. Theodore Roosevelt converted the room into a study in 1902, and in 1929 it became Lou Hoover's Monroe Room. Eleanor Roosevelt held her press conferences there until World War II, when the room became Winston Churchill's personal map room. Later, it became a sitting room again.

Mrs. Kennedy felt that a private conference room on the second floor would be of value to the President ("It's really to get the Cabinet out of the living room," she said candidly) and decided to restore it as such. A number of pieces of furniture used by President Andrew Johnson were returned to the room, along with a table associated with Grant and other mid-nineteenth-century presidents. The walls were covered with green velvet wallpaper, and a crystal chandelier that Grant had once placed in the East Room was hung over the table. Copies of treaties signed in the room over the years adorned the walls. It was in that newly refurbished room that President Kennedy signed the Nuclear Test Ban Treaty in 1963.

The television audience did not, of course, see the private quarters of the First Family, but Jacqueline Kennedy had made many changes there too. She had, for instance, turned Margaret Truman's old bedroom into a dining room, and the adjoining room into a kitchen, so that the First Family would not have to descend to the nonprivate first floor for meals.

One of Mrs. Kennedy's favorite rooms was the Lincoln Bedroom. There, Lincoln had held his Cabinet meetings and had signed the Emancipation Proclamation. In later years it became a bedroom and a bed that had been purchased for the White House by Lincoln had been installed there. It was President Truman who had decided to place other furniture associated with Lincoln in the room, and President Eisenhower had carried out the scheme. Mrs. Kennedy acquired additional appropriate pieces for the room, which was still dominated by the ornately carved bed with its high headboard. Later Jacqueline Kennedy recalled her feelings about the room:

Sometimes I used to stop and think about it all. I wondered, "What are we doing here" and "What are we going to be doing in a year or so?" I would go and sit in the Lincoln Room. It was the one room in the White House with a link to the past. It gave me great comfort. I love the Lincoln Room the most, even though it isn't really Lincoln's bedroom. But it has his things in it. When you see that great bed, it looks like a cathedral. To touch something I knew he had touched was a real link with him. The kind of peace I felt in that room was what you feel when going into a church. I used to sit in the Lincoln Room and I could really feel his strength. I'd sort of be talking to him.

Mrs. Kennedy's fondness for the Lincoln Bedroom heightened her belief that the entire White House should have the same historic aura. Her sense of closeness to Lincoln may also have helped her through those terrible days of November 1963, when President Kennedy was assassinated, and the country and the

In November 1963 the nation grieved again for a slain President. At Jacqueline Kennedy's request many details of her husband's funeral duplicated those of the Lincoln funeral in 1865: the coffin rested in the East Room on a replica of Lincoln's catafalque (left); windows, fireplaces, and even chandeliers were draped in black, and the room was lit by candles; an honor guard of servicemen kept constant vigil. In the photograph below, the black caisson, drawn by six matched grey horses, leaves the White House for the Capitol.

In 1967 President and Mrs. Lyndon B. Johnson entertained Díaz Ordaz, former President of Mexico, in the Yellow Oval Room (left). Vice President and Mrs. Hubert H. Humphrey are among those admiring a gift sword. At right, a few of the numerous antiwar pickets that plagued the Johnson administration march along Pennsylvania Avenue in front of the White House. Under Richard M. Nixon, the Green Room was completely redecorated (below).

world were plunged into despair. When Kennedy's body was brought back from Dallas to the East Room, Mrs. Kennedy asked that the funeral arrangements approximate as closely as possible those of Lincoln's rites almost one hundred years earlier. In that time of grief, there could be little comfort for the President's family, or for Americans who loved him. But it did help a little to recall Lincoln's death and to reflect that the nation had somehow survived even that great tragedy.

"Don't be frightened of this house," Mrs. Kennedy told her successor, Lady Bird Johnson, soon after the assassination, "some of the happiest years of my marriage have been spent here — you will be happy here." For a while, of course, the memory of the dead President was all-pervasive. Black mourning crepe hung over the doorways and on the chandeliers in the first-floor rooms; the flag over the mansion stayed at half-mast. References to "President Johnson" seemed unnatural and startling.

Eventually, however, the Johnsons began to feel free to impart their own style to the mansion. The President's earthy exuberance and the First Lady's graciousness created a Texas-style hospitality that was something new for the White House. The mansion was filled with guests and with activity, almost around the clock. In her book, *A White House Diary*, Lady Bird Johnson wrote about the dismaying lack of privacy in the Johnson White House. One night, after a long and busy day and evening, she had gone for a postmidnight swim in the pool and had then gone straight to the President's bedroom. Dressed in an old bathrobe, her hair still wet, she "opened the door and started into his bedroom. Aghast, I found it full of

men — Gregory Peck, Hugh O'Brian — ten or twelve more — with Lyndon on the table getting a rubdown and holding them in conversation at the same time. I shrieked and backed out. What a household! And what a moral to always have your hair combed and give that comfortable old bathrobe to the Goodwill charity organization."

Johnson worked hard and played hard, and always seemed to be the center of a whirlwind of activity. In his Oval Office, he had installed three television screens and two wire service machines, so that he would have immediate access to television and newspaper coverage of the day's events. He loved to make unexpected appearances at Lady Bird's White House functions, swooping in, saying a few words to the surprised assemblage, and swooping out again. Journalists reported his antics with his dogs, and when he tried to save money by urging that no unnecessary lights be turned on in the mansion, the press had a field day. One of Johnson's favorite recreations was walking down to the White House gates and shaking hands with delighted passersby through the bars.

White House entertainment during the Johnson years reflected the President's uninhibited enthusiasm for a good time among friends. He loved parties and whirled around the dance floor with almost every woman present. Much in keeping with the Johnson style was a county fair held on the White House lawn for the children of congressmen and other government officials. Lady Bird described the event:

There was a ferris wheel and a merry-go-round and a pony ring around the fountain and stands dispensing hot dogs, Coca-Cola, taffy apples, popcorn, and cotton

President Nixon's desk (left) dates to 1858. Nixon used it in the Capitol when he was Vice President, and brought it to his Oval Office in the West Wing when he became Chief Executive. Along the wall stand the flags of the armed services, with streamers representing major American campaigns. In the photo at right, the Nixons, with daughters Tricia and Julie and son-in-law David Eisenhower, gather for a meal in the second-floor family dining room. The cut-glass chandelier, dating from the eighteenth century, illuminates wallpaper depicting scenes from the Revolution.

candy. The view from the top of the ferris wheel of the White House grounds, dotted with red striped tents and about five hundred children, milling, running, laughing, was one I will never forget.

Although she concentrated on her own campaign to beautify America, Lady Bird followed Mrs. Kennedy's example in continuing to acquire items of historic and artistic interest for the White House. One such acquisition was a silver coffee urn that had belonged to John and Abigail Adams and had been used in the newly built mansion by its first occupants. Mrs. Johnson placed it in the Green Room. In that same parlor was displayed Monet's *Morning on the Seine*, presented to the White House by the Kennedy family in memory of the late President. Johnson issued an executive order making the post of White House Curator permanent and establishing an official Committee for the Preservation of the White House.

The two Johnson daughters, Lynda Bird and Luci Baines, like all other presidential daughters, found living in a goldfish bowl difficult. Both, however, managed to surmount the problems, and both became White House brides. Although Luci's wedding to Patrick Nugent took place in the National Shrine of the Immaculate Conception, the reception was held in the East Room; Lynda and Charles Robb later exchanged their vows in the same great hall, and cut their wedding cake with Captain Robb's Marine dress sword. Both young men served in Vietnam during their father-in-law's Presidency.

It is ironic that Lyndon Johnson, the most naturally outgoing of men, became, in the full term to which he was elected in 1964, an isolated President. Because of ever-increasing opposition to the war in Vietnam, Johnson was compelled, for his own safety, to withdraw more and more into the White House, where he could pursue the policies he believed to be right without danger from impassioned dissenters. Even in the White House, however, dissent could not be stilled; at various functions, guests unexpectedly gave voice to their opposition to the war. The nation's racial unrest was another divisive issue. After the assassination of Martin Luther King in 1968, riots broke out in Washington as in other American cities, and the violence came within a few blocks of the White House, which was guarded by armed troops. The image of the White House as a besieged fortress, in which the President was guarded from the people, was a new and tragic page in the history of the mansion and the nation.

Under Johnson's successor, Richard M. Nixon, life in the White House was more formal than it had been during the Johnson years, and in some respects less colorful. Anxious to bring as many Americans as possible into the Executive Mansion, the Nixons entertained more than 50,000 guests at receptions, dinners, and other functions during their first year alone. But since the President never danced, and did not really seem to enjoy parties, these events lacked the gaiety of Kennedy functions and the liveliness of the Johnson parties. A memorable exception was an affair honoring the seventieth birthday of composer Duke Ellington, whose father had been a part-time butler at the mansion during the Harding administration. Jazz rocked the East Room, and Nixon himself played "Happy Birthday" to Ellington on the great Steinway piano that is a permanent East Room fixture. Another successful party was the one given in 1970 in honor of Prince Charles and Princess Anne of Great Britain, with Tricia Nixon and Julie and David Eisenhower as host and hostesses. As White House guests, Charles and Anne were assigned the Lincoln and Queens' bedrooms, the same suites that had been used by their parents in 1957 and by their grandparents in 1939.

The series of Sunday religious services that the Nixons instituted at the White House received a mixed reaction from the nation's press. Conducted in the East Room by clergymen of various denominations and faiths, these services were held monthly; each was attended by about three hundred guests. Some critics pointed out that the services contradicted the principle of separation of Church and State, but those who attended found them moving and uplifting.

Another Nixon innovation got not a mixed reaction but a totally negative one. Impressed by the uniforms of the men guarding various official residences in Europe, the President ordered new garb for the White House guards. But the sloped black plastic hats and heavily braided new uniforms made the guards, as *Life* magazine pointed out, "instantly reminiscent of players in a Rudolf Friml operetta, banana republic palace guards, full-dress Lippizaner horsemen, and even head ushers at the Roxy."

Under Patricia Nixon's supervision, the permanent White House collection of art and antiques continued to expand. Threadbare and shabby after almost ten years of heavy use, the Red, Green, and Blue rooms were refurbished, and the ground-floor Map Room — F.D.R.'s communications headquarters during World War II — was transformed into a comfortable confer-

The presidential seal is prominently displayed on the first floor, above the entrance to the Blue Room.
  Overleaf:
The South Portico of the White House is framed by splashing fountains amidst a riot of spring tulips.

ence room with American Chippendale furnishings. Thomas Jefferson's traveling desk and a number of fine paintings were among the interesting features of the room, which was first used officially in 1970 for a meeting between President Nixon and former President Lyndon B. Johnson.

In the colonnade connecting the mansion to the West Wing, the swimming pool that had been built for F.D.R. was boarded over to make more room for the 1,500 newsmen accredited to the White House. For his Oval Office in the executive wing, Nixon chose the carved mahogany desk that he had used at the Capitol during his vice-presidential years. A Charles Willson Peale portrait of Washington, a bust of Lincoln, and a collection of porcelain birds were selected to decorate the office. From his desk, the President could look out at the lovely rose garden, where his daughter Tricia married Edward Cox in 1971 in the first White House wedding held outdoors.

Actually, President Nixon used the famous Oval Office primarily for various official functions. He found that a far less formidable office in the Old Executive Office Building next door to the White House was more conducive to work. And when he had an important speech to work on, he often slipped away to the small sitting room off the Lincoln Bedroom, where a shabby, overstuffed modern chair — Nixon's favorite — had been placed for him among the Victorian furnishings.

Obviously the White House is as difficult to work in efficiently as it is impossible to live in with any degree of privacy. Yet it remains a unique edifice, symbolic as is no other building of the history and high ideals of the American Republic. No man who lives and works there can fail to be inspired, to some degree at least, by the knowledge that John Adams, Thomas Jefferson, Andrew Jackson, Abraham Lincoln, Woodrow Wilson, the two Roosevelts, and other great men have lived within the same walls and shouldered the burdens of the Presidency. Dwight Eisenhower spoke for all American presidents when he summed up his feelings about the mansion:

My conviction is that the White House has been and should always remain a place to be venerated by its occupants as well as by all Americans. I believe that because of the White House's meaning for America — and assuming its stability in structure and surroundings — a visitor of the generation of 2050 or 3050 should be able to gain from it the same sense of humility, pride, reverence, and history that my wife and I felt every day of the years we were privileged to live in it. For the White House is not just a well-run home for the Chief Executive; it is a living story of past pioneering, struggles, wars, innovations, and a growing America. I like to think of it as a symbol of freedom and of the hopes and future accomplishments of her people.

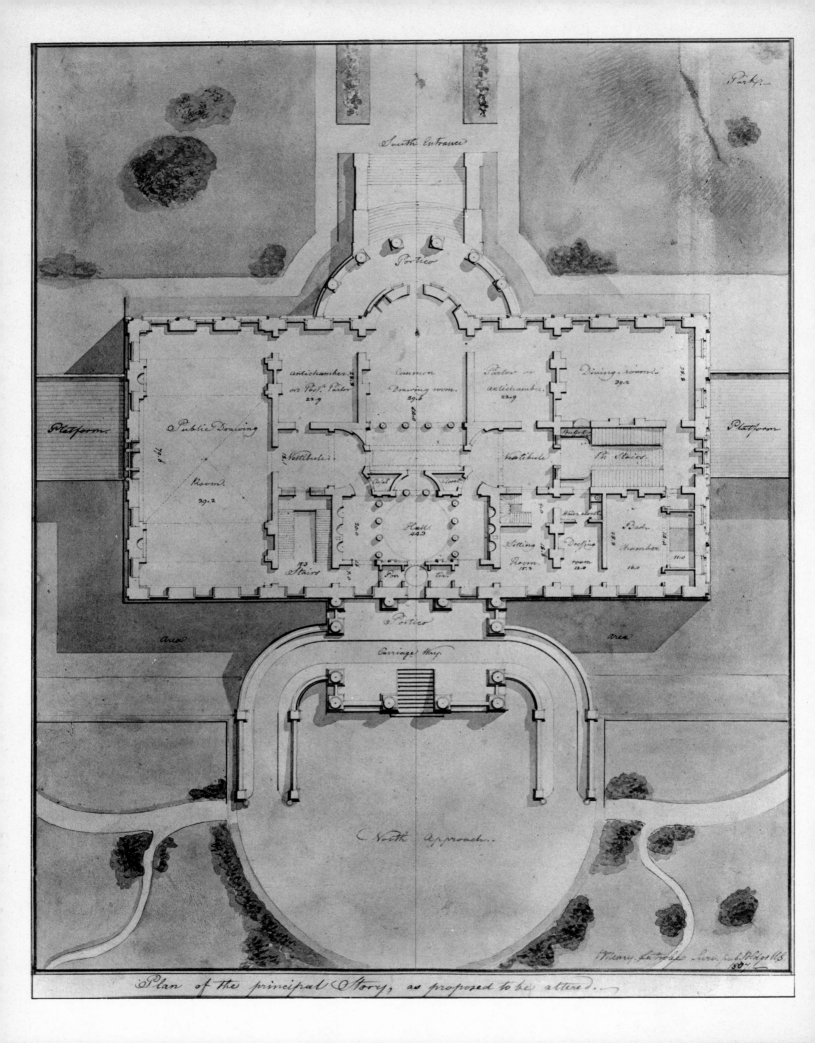

South Entrance

Portico

Park

Platform

Platform

antichamber.
or Poet's Parlor
22.9

Common
Drawing room
29.6

Parlor or
antichamber.
22.9

Dining room
39.2

Public Drawing

Room.
39.2

Vestibule

Closet

Closet

Vestibule

Pr. Stairs

Buffet

Stairs

Hall
44.3

Sitting
Room
15.3

Dressing
room
12.0

Bed.
Chamber
16.0

11.0

Fr.   ter.

Stairs

Portico

Area

Area

Carriage Way.

North Approach.

B. Henry Latrobe Surve

Plan of the principal Story, as proposed to be altered.

WHITE HOUSE MEMORIES

*The literature of life in the White House began with the witty letters of Mrs.
John Adams, the first President's wife to preside over the Executive Mansion.
Although her husband had assured her that the mansion was "habitable," Abigail
Adams found that the house left much to be desired. Shortly after moving into
the White House in November 1800, she sent this candid report to her daughter,
Abigail Smith.*

My Dear Child,

I arrived here on Sunday last, without meeting any accident worth noticing,
except losing ourselves when we left Baltimore, and going eight or nine miles
on the Frederick road, by which means we were obliged to go the other eight
through woods, where we wandered two hours without finding a guide, or
the path. Fortunately, a straggling black came up with us, and we engaged
him as a guide, to extricate us out of our difficulty; but woods are all you see,
from Baltimore until you reach *the city*, which is only so in name. . . . In the
city there are buildings enough, if they were compact and finished, to accommodate Congress and those attached to it; but as they are, and scattered as
they are, I see no great comfort in them. . . . The house is upon a grand and
superb scale, requiring about thirty servants to attend and keep the apartments in proper order, and perform the ordinary business of the house and
stables; an establishment very well proportioned to the President's salary.
The lighting the apartments, from the kitchen to parlours and chambers is
a tax indeed; and the fires we are obliged to keep to secure us from daily
agues is another very cheering comfort. To assist us in this great castle, and
render less attendance necessary, bells are wholly wanting, not one single one
being hung through the whole house, and promises are all you can obtain.
This is so great an inconvenience, that I know not what to do, or how to do.
The ladies from Georgetown and in the city have many of them visited me.
Yesterday I returned fifteen visits, — but such a place as Georgetown appears,
— why, our Milton is beautiful. But no comparisons; — if they will put me
up some bells, and let me have wood enough to keep fires, I design to be
pleased. I could content myself almost anywhere three months; but, surrounded with forests, can you believe that wood is not to be had, because
people cannot be found to cut and cart it! Briesler entered into a contract
with a man to supply him with wood. A small part, a few cords only, has he
been able to get. Most of that was expended to dry the walls of the house
before we came in, and yesterday the man told him it was impossible for him
to procure it to be cut and carted. He has had recourse to coals; but we
cannot get grates made and set. We have, indeed, come into *a new country*.

You must keep all this to yourself, and, when asked how I like it, say that
I write you the situation is beautiful, which is true. The house is made
habitable, but there is not a single apartment finished, and all withinside,
except the plastering, has been done since Briesler came. We have not the
least fence, yard, or other convenience, without, and the great unfinished
audience-room I make a drying-room of, to hang up the clothes in. The
principal stairs are not up, and will not be this winter. Six chambers are
made comfortable; two are occupied by the President and Mr. Shaw; two
lower rooms, one for a common parlour, and one for a levee-room. Up stairs
there is the oval room, which is designed for the drawingroom, and has the
crimson furniture in it. It is a very handsome room now; but, when completed, it will be beautiful. If the twelve years, in which this place has been

considered as the future seat of government, had been improved, as they would have been if in New England, very many of the present inconveniences would have been removed. It is a beautiful spot, capable of every improvement, and, the more I view it, the more I am delighted with it.

ABIGAIL ADAMS
Letter to her daughter, 1800

Later first ladies were spared the hardships that Abigail Adams endured in the winter of 1800–1801, but life in the mansion continued to be filled with drama. Perhaps the most critical moment in the building's history came in August 1814, when British forces marched on Washington during the War of 1812. Dolley Madison, best-known for her abilities as a hostess and social leader, faced the danger with cool courage. She gave her sister the following day-by-day account of life in the threatened capital.

Tuesday Augt 23d 1814.

Dear Sister, — My husband left me yesterday morng to join Gen. Winder. He enquired anxiously whether I had courage, or firmness to remain in the President's house until his return, on the morrow, or succeeding day and on my assurance that I had no fear but for him and the success of our army, he left me, beseeching me to take care of myself, and of the cabinet papers, public and private. I have since recd two despatches from him written with a pencil; the last is alarming, because he desires I should be ready at a moment's warning to enter my carriage and leave the city; that the enemy seemed stronger than had been reported, and that it might happen they would reach the city, with intention to destroy it. . . . I am accordingly ready; I have pressed as many cabinet papers into trunks as to fill one carriage; our private property must be sacrificed, as it is impossible to procure wagons for its transportation. I am determined not to go myself until I see Mr. Madison safe, and he can accompany me, — as I hear of much hostility towards him. . . . French John (a faithful domestic,) with his usual activity and resolution, offers to spike the cannon at the gate, and to lay a train of powder which would blow up the British should they enter the house. To the last proposition I positively object, without being able, however, to make him understand why all advantages in war may not be taken.

Wednesday morng twelve o'clock. — Since sunrise I have been turning my spy glass in every direction and watching with unwearied anxiety, hoping to discover the approach of my dear husband and his friends; but, alas, I can descry only groups of military wandering in all directions, as if there was a lack of arms, or of spirit to fight for their own firesides.

Three o'clock. — Will you believe it, my sister? We have had a battle, or skirmish near Bladensburg, and I am still here within sound of the cannon! Mr Madison comes not; may God protect him! Two messengers, covered with dust, come to bid me fly; but I wait for him. . . . At this late hour, a wagon has been procured; I have had it filled with the plate and most valuable portable articles belonging to the house; whether it will reach its destination, the Bank of Maryland, or fall into the hands of British soldiery, events must determine.

Our friend Mr Carroll, has come to hasten my departure, and is in a very bad humor with me because I insist on waiting until the large picture

These souvenir buttons were issued to celebrate George Washington's first inaugural, March 4, 1789. The button at top right combines the initials of the President with those of the thirteen states. The other buttons show an American eagle, Washington's initials again, and his profile.

139

of Gen. Washington is secured, and it requires to be unscrewed from the wall. This process was found too tedious for these perilous moments; I have ordered the frame to be broken, and the canvass taken out; it is done, — and the precious portrait placed in the hands of two gentlemen of New York, for safe keeping. And now, dear sister, I must leave this house, or the retreating army will make me a prisoner in it, by filling up the road I am directed to take. When I shall again write to you, or where I shall be tomorrow, I cannot tell!!

DOLLEY MADISON
Letters to her sister, 1814

The White House was rebuilt after the British assault of 1814, and the mansion became a peaceful home for first families in the next decades. As American prestige grew, Washington became a more sophisticated and cosmopolitan city. Perhaps no White House hostess enjoyed the capital's social life in these years as much as did Priscilla Cooper Tyler, daughter-in-law of John Tyler. An actress before her marriage to Robert Tyler, Priscilla found the Executive Mansion a perfect stage for her talents. When Count Henri Bertrand, a former aide of Napoleon Bonaparte, visited Washington, Priscilla proudly shared her triumphs with her sister.

You say you hear Bertrand is coming to this country. My dear, he has come, seen, and conquered — or he has come, been seen, and I have been conquered. The Marshal arrived during the President's absence in Virginia, and the whole duty of entertaining him fell upon me. To be sure, Mr. Tyler [her husband, Robert] is here, but he is only Prince Consort. Of course I was equal to the situation. He arrived on Saturday evening, and sent me word asking at what hour I could see him, and at what hour he might call. I appointed eight o'clock, it being then seven. I immediately sent for the officers of the Cabinet and was surrounded by them when the old hero arrived, accompanied by his suite. He bowed to the very ground, and I curtseyed quite as low. I cannot convey to you any idea of how charmingly I received him. The hour that he spent, he spent in complimenting me in French and English rather jumbled together, while I returned his compliments in the same eccentric mixture of languages.

At last, after a flourishing speech and squeezing my hand, with a second low bow over it, he departed, followed by his suite, each giving a profound obeisance. I could not resist the impulse, and as the last mustachioed Frenchman left the room, I turned a pirouette on one foot, and then dropping a low curtsey, said I begged the cabinet's pardon; whereat Mr. Tyler was exceedingly wrathy, though everyone else said it was the sweetest thing I had done all evening.

The Marshal was to leave the next morning, Sunday, but I sent him an invitation for Monday evening. You should see the note of acceptance he wrote. I have it in my book of autographs. He had intended leaving, but my gracious invitation was not to be resisted. I had such a short time to accomplish a great deal, but, my usual administrative powers called into activity, I succeeded in doing all I wished to do: sent out two hundred invitations to the *creme de la creme* of Washington society.

At eight o'clock the party was assembled, formed of the very prettiest

The invitation below announces a ball in honor of President-elect Andrew Jackson that was to be held in Nashville on December 23, 1828. But when the day came there was little cause for rejoicing; Jackson's wife had died the night before. The campaign ribbon at right and the spoon below bear the images that swept William Henry Harrison into the White House in 1840: a log cabin and a barrel of hard cider. Actually a well-born Ohio planter, Harrison was portrayed as a simple backwoodsman.

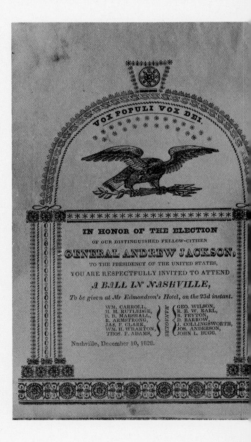

girls and the nicest people I could collect. All the officers of the army and navy appeared in their uniforms, the diplomatic corps in full court costume. I stood at the head of the blue center room near the window. As the Marshal arrived and walked through the hall, the band struck up the Marseillaise. The guests fell back on either side of the end of the room, leaving a wide path for Bertrand to advance to where Josephine — I mean, I — stood surrounded by the Cabinet. To describe the reverences he made, followed by his son and each of his suite in turn would be vain. I returned them with Grandmama's old-fashioned curtseys, such as must have existed in the days of the Empire. Soon after his arrival the band struck up for dancing. I only danced twice — once to open the ball with Count Bertrand, the Marshal's son, and once again with his Aide de Camp, at his request . . . two young Frenchmen composed entirely of pantaloons and mustaches.

For the rest of the evening my guests demanded my attention. No party ever went off better. Father with his usual kindness had given me *carte blanche* before he left. My supper was splendid. (It is so easy to entertain at other people's expense.) The prettiest things on the table were the pyramids of pomegranates with their skins peeled off and the Malaga grapes. They looked like rubies and emeralds. . . . Nothing was on the long principal table but things of the most aerial, glittering description. Meats of all descriptions were banished to the side tables; and altogether everything was as plentiful and brilliant as I could make it. I personally directed everything. When the Marshal led me in to supper, he seemed completely overcome, and putting his hand over his heart, said, "Ah, madame . . . all zis for me?"

The only *contretemps* that occurred was that I gave him with a sweet smile a most splendid-looking sugar plum without looking at the picture on it, which I afterwards discovered to my horror to be that of an ape.

The old gentleman did not leave until all the guests had departed, and then made a long speech of adieu, saying at the end, "I zink vous etes charmante, madame . . . I zink you one vary good woman . . . and all your people must lof you. Adieu. Madame, I shall never forget you."

Then saluting my hand in the most chivalrous, French, respectful, delicious manner, he left me alone in my glory.

PRISCILLA COOPER TYLER
*Letter to
her sister,* 1843

AN ELECTION
IN WARTIME

Twenty years after Priscilla Tyler's reception for Bertrand, the White House was again in danger. One of the most vivid accounts of life in Washington during the Civil War is the diary of John Hay, Abraham Lincoln's secretary; and some of the most fascinating entries in this journal were made in November 1864. General George McClellan, the Democrats' "peace" candidate, was a serious threat to Lincoln. Hay recorded events on election night as well as Lincoln's startling revelation to the Cabinet when his reelection had been confirmed three days later.

[November 8, 1864]

The house has been still and almost deserted today. Everybody in Washington, not at home voting, seems ashamed of it and stays away from the President.

I was talking with him to-day. He said, "It is a little singular that I, who am not a vindictive man, should have always been before the people for election in canvasses marked for their bitterness: always but once; when I came to Congress it was a quiet time. But always besides that the contests in which I have been prominent have been marked with great rancor."

At noon Butler [Benjamin Butler who had been sent to New York] sent a despatch simply saying, "The quietest city ever seen". . . .

Hoffman sent a very cheering despatch giving a rose-coloured estimate of the forenoon's voting in Baltimore. "I shall be glad if that holds," said the President. . . .

At night, at 7 o'clock we started over to the War Department to spend the evening. . . .

The night was rainy, steamy and dark. We splashed through the grounds to the side door of the War Department where a soaked and smoking sentinel was standing in his own vapor with his huddled-up frame covered with a rubber cloak. Inside a half-dozen idle orderlies, up-stairs the clerks of the telegraph. As the President entered they handed him a despatch from Forney [John W. Forney of Philadelphia and Washington] claiming ten thousand Union majority in Philadelphia. "Forney is a little excitable." Another comes from Felton, Baltimore, giving us "15,000 in the city, 5,000 in the state. All Hail, Free Maryland." That is superb. A message from Rice [candidate in Massachusetts] to Fox [Secretary of the Navy and Chief Clerk of the Navy Department], followed instantly by one from Sumner to Lincoln, claiming Boston by 5,000, and Rice's & Hooper's elections by majorities of 4,000 apiece. A magnificent advance on the chilly dozens of 1862. . . .

The President sent over the first fruits to Mrs. Lincoln. He said, "She is more anxious than I."

We went into the Secretary's room. Mr Wells and Fox soon came in. They were especially happy over the election of Rice, regarding it as a great triumph for the Navy Department. Says Fox, "There are two fellows that have been especially malignant to us, and retribution has come upon them both. . . ." "You have more of that feeling of personal resentment than I," said Lincoln. "Perhaps I may have too little of it, but I never thought it paid. A man has not time to spend half his life in quarrels. If any man ceases to attack me, I never remember the past against him. . . ."

Despatches kept coming in all the evening showing a splendid triumph in Indiana, showing steady, small gains all over Pennsylvania, enough to give a fair majority this time on the home vote. Guesses from New York and Albany which boiled down to about the estimated majority against us in the city, 35,000, and left the result in the State still doubtful. . . .

Towards midnight we had supper, provided by Eckert [Thomas Eckert, the War Department's chief of the telegraph section]. The President went awkwardly and hospitably to work shovelling out the fried oysters. He was most agreeable and genial all the evening in fact. Fox was abusing the coffee for being so hot — saying quaintly, it kept hot all the way down to the bottom of the cup as a piece of ice staid cold till you finished eating it.

We got later in the evening a scattering despatch from the West, giving us Michigan, one from Fox promising Missouri certainly. . . .

Capt Thomas came up with a band about half-past two, and made some music and a small hifalute.

The President answered from the window with rather unusual dignity and effect & we came home. . . .

HENRY CLAY

THE PEOPLE'S CHOICE

THE PRIDE OF AMERICA.

FRELINGHUYSEN.

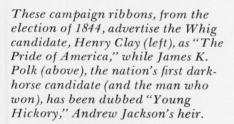

These campaign ribbons, from the election of 1844, advertise the Whig candidate, Henry Clay (left), as "The Pride of America," while James K. Polk (above), the nation's first dark-horse candidate (and the man who won), has been dubbed "Young Hickory," Andrew Jackson's heir.

[November 11, 1864]

At the meeting of the Cabinet today, the President took out a paper from his desk and said, "Gentlemen, do you remember last summer I asked you all to sign your names to the back of a paper of which I did not show you the inside? This is it. Now, Mr. Hay, see if you can get this open without tearing it?" He had pasted it up in so singular style that it required some cutting to get it open. He then read as follows: . . .

This morning, as for some days past, it seems exceedingly probable that this Administration will not be reelected. Then it will be my duty to so cooperate with the President elect, as to save the Union between the election and the inauguration; as he will have secured his election on such ground that he cannot possibly save it afterwards.

A. LINCOLN

. . . The President said, "You will remember that this was written at a time (6 days before the Chicago nominating Convention) when as yet we had no adversary, and seemed to have no friends. I then solemnly resolved on the course of action indicated above. I resolved, in case of the election of General McClellan, being certain that he would be the candidate, that I would see him and talk matters over with him. I would say, "General, the election has demonstrated that you are stronger, have more influence with the American people than I. Now let us together, you with your influence and I with all the executive power of the Government, try to save the country. You raise as many troops as you possibly can for this final trial, and I will devote all my energies to assisting and finishing the war."

Seward [the Secretary of State] said, "And the General would answer you 'Yes, Yes;' and the next day when you saw him again and pressed these views upon him, he would say, 'Yes, Yes;' & so on forever, and would have done nothing at all."

"At least," added Lincoln, "I should have done my duty and have stood clear before my own conscience."

JOHN HAY
*Diaries and Letters
of John Hay,* 1864

BURDENED DAUGHTER, PRIVILEGED SON

The end of the Civil War did not bring peace or happiness to the White House. Andrew Johnson, Lincoln's successor, was the object of congressional impeachment proceedings, and Mrs. Johnson's ill health forced her daughter Martha Patterson to assume the duties of official hostess. A friend of Mrs. Patterson recalled a visit to the mansion in the last days of the Johnson administration when Martha Patterson's usual poise faltered for a minute, and she made a candid admission, revealing something of the terrible strain she had borne during her father's troubled term in office.

Late in the afternoon, I was sitting in the cheerful room occupied by the invalid mother, when Mrs. Patterson came for me to go and see the table. The last state dinner was to be given this night, and the preparation for the occasion had been commensurate with those of former occasions.

I looked at the invalid, whose feet had never crossed the apartment to which we were going, and by whom the elegant entertainments, over which her daughters presided, were totally unenjoyed. Through the hall, and down the stairway, I followed my hostess, and stood beside her in the grand old room.

It was a beautiful, and altogether a rare scene, which I viewed in the quiet light of that closing winter day. . . . From the heavy curtains depending from the lofty windows, to the smallest ornament in the room, all was ornate and consistent. I could not but contrast this vision of grandeur with the delicate, child-like form of the woman who watched me with a quiet smile, as I enjoyed this evidence of her taste, and appreciation of the beautiful. All day she had watched over the movements of those engaged in the arrangement of this room, and yet so unobtrusive had been her presence, and so systematically had she planned, that no confusion occurred in the complicated domestic machinery. . . . All was ready and complete, and when we passed from the room, there was still time for rest before the hour named in the cards of invitation. . . . It was almost twilight, as we entered the East Room, and its sombreness and wondrous size struck me forcibly. The hour for strangers and visitors had passed, and we felt at liberty to wander, in our old-fashioned way, up and down its great length.

It was softly raining, we discovered, as we peered through the window, and a light fringe of mist hung over the trees in the grounds. The feeling of balmy comfort one feels in watching it rain, from the window of a cozy room, was intensified by the associations of this historic place, and the sadness of time was lost in the outreachings of eternity. . . . Mrs. Patterson was the first to note the flight of time, and, as we turned, to leave with the past the hour it claimed, her grave face lighted up with a genuinely happy expression, as she said: "I am glad this is the last entertainment; it suits me better to be quiet, and in my own home. Mother is not able to enjoy these things. Belle is too young, and I am indifferent to them — so it is well it is almost over."

MARY CLEMMER AMES
Ten Years in Washington, 1876

One of the weightier souvenirs of the 1848 election campaign was the cast-iron stove above, decorated with the profile of General Zachary Taylor. The 1860 campaign featured the "Union" ribbon below and the homemade Lincoln ribbon at right, cut from a strip of leather, crudely lettered, and decorated with a portrait of the Republican candidate.

The Johnsons left the scene of their public and personal sorrows in 1869, and the White House became the home of Ulysses S. Grant. An enormously popular military hero, Grant brought four lively children to brighten the old mansion. Jesse, the youngest of the Grants, found that a President's son could benefit from his father's position in very special ways.

In the early days in my new home the only sorrows I ever knew in the White House came to me. I possessed all the normal small boy's fondness for a dog and acquired several in rapid succession, only to have each, in turn, die. Over each demise my grief was bitter. Then some one presented me with a magnificent Newfoundland. When this dog came, father called the White House steward. He asked no questions, made no accusations.

"Jesse has a new dog," he said, simply. "You may have noticed that his former pets have been peculiarly unfortunate. When this dog dies every employee in the White House will be at once discharged."

"Faithful" was the name I gave this dog, and he, and one or two more I acquired later, lived during the remainder of our stay in the White House. . . .

Other than dogs, I had few pets in the White House. At one time I was filled with the desire to keep pigeons, but it appeared that at an earlier time

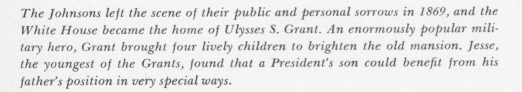

144

Tad Lincoln had been fired by the same ambition, and that the caretakers of the Treasury and other public buildings were still striving to exterminate the hardy survivors of Tad's breeding. For me pigeons were taboo. . . .

But though my pets were comparatively few, my other interests were multitudinous. It was in the early days of my life in the White House that I became interested in stamp collecting.

Boys never change. I am convinced that the first cave boy was a collector. The mania for stamp collecting came upon me with the thrill of a great discovery, and for a time it held me in a gripping fervor of enthusiasm that overwhelmed every other interest. No one had ever imagined such a stamp collection as I would gather.

Then I came upon the advertisement of one Anthony J. Foster, of Milk Street, Boston. This advertisement offered a large assortment of foreign stamps for five dollars. I had never possessed five dollars at one time. To me it was a vast sum. It did not occur to me that there was any possibility of acquiring such wealth except by saving it. So I said nothing of my ambition to anyone, save to my cousin. He and I at once decided that there would be no more candy or soda water until we were possessed of the price of that assortment of stamps.

And at last, at the cost of much self-denial and after an interminable time, the five dollars was amassed and on its way to Boston. Then, with impatience that reckoned not of distance or train schedules, I looked for the arrival of the stamps. I presume now that to my impatience the dragging hours became days and that I lost hope of the arrival of the stamps or the return of the money long before delivery could have reasonably been expected. And in my anxiety and fear I consulted my stanch friend, Kelly.

Kelly was a big-bodied and bigger-hearted member of the Washington police force, detailed on special duty at the White House. In my eyes, Kelly, next to my father, was the greatest man in Washington.

"Sure, ye better tell your father about it, Jesse," was Kelly's advice.

And so I took my trouble to father.

"What do you wish me to do, my dear boy?" asked father.

I had been thinking about this, too.

"I thought you might have the Secretary of State, or the Secretary of War, or Kelly, write a letter," I suggested.

"Hum-m!" mused father. "A matter of this importance requires consideration. Suppose you come to the Cabinet meeting, to-morrow, and we will take the matter up there."

Promptly on the hour I presented myself at the Cabinet meeting. Hamilton Fish of New York was then Secretary of State, and William W. Belknap of Iowa Secretary of War. Both were great friends of mine.

"Jesse has a matter he wishes to bring before you, gentlemen," said father.

Breathlessly I told my story, ending with the suggestion that either the Secretary of State, the Secretary of War, or Kelly write a letter.

"This is plainly a matter for the State Department to attend to," said Mr. Fish.

To this Mr. Belknap promptly took exception, declaring it his intention, as head of the War Department, to act at once.

Followed a general debate, in which the other Cabinet members stood solidly for Kelly. I shall never forget with what interest I listened to impassioned speeches in which Kelly's virtues, his power and influence, were extolled. He was declared to have wider powers than the Constitution bestowed upon either the Department of State or the War Department, and his personal ability and influence were proclaimed to be greater than that of the Secretaries who sought to usurp his prerogatives. When the question was put to vote, Mr. Fish and Mr. Belknap voted for their respective departments, but the rest of the Cabinet voted for Kelly. Then the decision was formally announced and I went down stairs to find Kelly.

I can see Kelly now, as he sat doubled over at a small desk, writing that letter on the stationery of the "Executive Mansion" — so headed at that time — the sweat standing out on his forehead, his great fingers gripping the pen.

At father's suggestion, I made a copy before mailing the original letter. It read:

I am a Capitol Policeman. I can arrest anybody, anywhere, at any time, for anything. I want you to send those stamps to Jesse Grant right at once.

signed, Kelly,

Capitol Policeman.

A dozen times the following day I made anxious inquiry for the reply to Kelly's letter. In due time the stamps arrived. As I remember, that five-dollar assortment exceeded our expectations.

JESSE R. GRANT
In the Days of My Father General Grant, 1925

T. R.'S BROOD

In 1901, the White House became the home of the most exuberant tenants in its history: Theodore and Edith Roosevelt and their six children. The President enjoyed the mansion as much as or more than did his sons and daughters. When his second son, Kermit, left for boarding school, Roosevelt dictated letters like this one so that the boy could still share in the delights of life on Pennsylvania Avenue.

Tom Quartz is certainly the cunningest kitten I have ever seen. He is always playing pranks on Jack [one of the Roosevelt dogs] and I get very nervous lest Jack should grow too irritated. The other evening they were both in the library — Jack sleeping before the fire — Tom Quartz scampering about, an exceedingly playful little wild creature — which is about what he is. He would race across the floor and then jump upon the curtains or play with the tassels. Suddenly he spied Jack and galloped up to him. Jack, looking exceedingly sullen and shame-faced, jumped out of the way and got upon the sofa, where Tom Quartz instantly jumped upon him again. Jack suddenly shifted to the other sofa where Tom Quartz again went after him. Then Jack started for the door, while Tom made a rapid turn under the sofa and around the table and just as Jack reached the door leaped on his hind quarters. Jack bounded forward and away and the two went tandem out of the room — Jack not reappearing at all; and after about five minutes Tom Quartz stalked solemnly back.

Another evening the next Speaker of the House, Mr. Cannon, an exceedingly solemn, elderly gentleman with chin whiskers, who certainly does not look to be of a playful nature, came to call upon me. He is a great friend of mine and we sat talking over what our policies for the session should be until about eleven o'clock; and when he went I accompanied him to the head of the stairs. He had gone about half way down when Tom Quartz strolled by, his tail erect and very fluffy. He spied Mr. Cannon going down the stairs,

jumped to the conclusion that he was a playmate escaping, and raced after him, suddenly grasping him by the leg the way he does Archie and Quentin when they play hide and seek with him; then loosening his hold, he tore down stairs ahead of Mr. Cannon, who eyed him with iron calm and not one particle of surprise.

From now until the 4th of March my hands will be full. I am very anxious to get some action about the trusts as well as the Philippine measures, the army relief measures, the bill for going on with the building of the navy, and the Cuban reciprocity treaty — and I am having my hands full about them all. However, I am accustomed to both work and worry and I manage to have a pretty good time in spite of everything.

Ethel has reluctantly gone back to boarding school. It is just after lunch and Dulany is cutting my hair while I dictate this to Mr. Loeb. I left mother lying on the sofa and reading aloud to Quentin, who as usual has hung himself over the back of the sofa in what I should personally regard as an exceedingly uncomfortable attitude to listen to literature. Archie we shall not see until this evening, when he will suddenly challenge me either to a race or a bear play, and if neither invitation is accepted then will propose that I tell a pig story or else read aloud from the Norse folk tales.

THEODORE ROOSEVELT
Letter to his son, 1903

A BEGINNING AND AN ENDING

When the Roosevelts vacated the White House in 1909, their successors seemed assured of an equally pleasant stay in the mansion. William Howard Taft was Theodore Roosevelt's friend and protégé, and the jovial Secretary of War inherited much of the Rough Rider's popularity and prestige. Mrs. Taft's account of her first twenty-four hours in the White House shows her pride and delight in her new role as First Lady.

Some time before the Inauguration, indeed shortly after Mr. Taft's election, President Roosevelt expressed a desire that we should dine with him and Mrs. Roosevelt on the evening of the third of March and spend that night in the White House as their guests. This was breaking a precedent, but it was Mr. Roosevelt's plan for bidding us a warm welcome to the post which he was about to vacate, and my husband accepted with grateful appreciation. My impression is that neither Mrs. Roosevelt nor I would have suggested such an arrangement for this particular evening, but, it having been made for us, we naturally acquiesced.

The third of March, a stormy day, was filled with innumerable minor engagements and small incidents, with instructions and counter-instructions and, especially, with weather predictions and counter-predictions, so it was not until shortly before eight o'clock that Mr. Taft and I, having dressed for dinner, arrived at the White House. The other guests at the dinner were Senator and Mrs. Lodge, Senator and Mrs. Root, Admiral and Mrs. Cowles, Mr. and Mrs. Nicholas Longworth and Miss Mabel Boardman.

Now there is always bound to be a sadness about the end of an administration, no matter how voluntarily the retiring President may leave office, no matter how welcome the new President and his family may be. Mrs. Roosevelt seemed depressed, not, I am sure, over the prospect of leaving the White House, — Presidents' wives are always given plenty of time to prepare them-

The ribbons at left, somber mementos of the Presidency, were issued to commemorate the deaths of James A. Garfield (top), cut down by an assassin's bullet in 1881, and of former President Ulysses S. Grant (bottom), who died of cancer in 1885.

selves for that event, — but for other reasons which one easily could surmise. Her husband and son were about to start for a long and, possibly, dangerous trip into the jungles of Africa, and she was looking forward to a year of anxiety. She was leaving a full and busy life; she had occupied her high position for nearly eight years, during which she had made a host of friends, and a great number of them had called during the afternoon to say farewell and to express their deep regret at her departure. I knew of all these things, realised their depressing effect and sympathised with her deeply. The President and Mr. Taft, seconded by other guests, did their best with stories and conversation, made as general as possible, to lighten the occasion, but their efforts [were] not entirely successful.

As my husband had an engagement to attend a "smoker" which was being given him at the New Willard Hotel by a large gathering of Yale men, the party broke up very early and, as soon as the last of the guests had gone, I went immediately to my rooms. We had been assigned to the suite in the southeast corner, known in the White House as the Blue Bedroom.

The Blue Bedroom gave me food for interesting reflection. Conspicuous, under the mantel against the side wall, I found, on a bronze plate, the following inscription . . . "In this room Abraham Lincoln signed the Emancipation Proclamation of January 1, 1863, whereby four million slaves were given their freedom and slavery forever prohibited in these United States." It is only a state bedroom now, having been made so by the plans of the McKim restoration which was accomplished during the Roosevelt administration, but it was once Lincoln's Cabinet room, a room in which he lived through many terrible days during the Civil War. It seemed strange to spend my first night in the White House surrounded by such ghosts. I went to bed reasonably early, hoping that I might have a good, long sleep and get up refreshed and ready for an eventful day. But the press of circumstances was against me. My mind was never more wide awake. In spite of my determination to rest, I went carefully over the whole Inaugural programme. . . .

There was nobody at the White House to bid us welcome [after the inaugural ceremonies the following day] except the official staff and some of our own guests. But it didn't matter. There is never any ceremony about moving into the White House. You just drive up and walk in, — and there you are. The aides and ushers who greeted us at the entrance, treated our occupation of our new residence so much as a matter of course that I could not help but feel something as Cinderella must have felt when her mice footmen bowed her into her coach and four and behaved just as if they had conducted her to a Court Ball every night of her life. I stood for a moment over the great brass seal, bearing the national coat-of-arms, which is sunk in the floor in the middle of the entrance hall. "The Seal of the President of the United States," I read around the border, and now — that meant my husband!

But I could not linger long because my duties as a hostess began at once. I was not unused to the accepted regulations of official life, so, in spite of a slight feeling that the whole thing was unreal, I was not embarrassed as I walked into the great dining-room and took my place by the door to receive guests for the first time as mistress of the White House.

HELEN H. TAFT
Recollections of Full Years, 1914

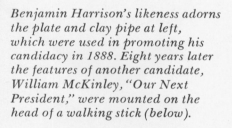

Benjamin Harrison's likeness adorns the plate and clay pipe at left, which were used in promoting his candidacy in 1888. Eight years later the features of another candidate, William McKinley, "Our Next President," were mounted on the head of a walking stick (below).

Mrs. Taft's bright hopes were to be disappointed. The First Lady suffered a stroke from which she never completely recovered, while her husband alienated his former mentor and was opposed by Roosevelt's "Bull Moose" candidacy in 1912. Inauguration day, 1913, was a poignant occasion for the Taft family. Irwin ("Ike") Hoover, chief usher of the White House, told the story in matter-of-fact fashion. To Hoover, who spent forty years at the Executive Mansion, the transfer of power from William Howard Taft to Woodrow Wilson — bizarre as it seems in retrospect — seemed "typical."

Mrs. Taft and Miss Helen had watched the departure [of Taft and Wilson for the Capitol] from the latter's bedroom on the second floor. They were entirely alone, so what their feelings were can only be surmised. Mrs. Taft had arranged beforehand to leave at eleven o'clock to go to the home of her sister . . . and there to be joined later by Mr. Taft and proceed to the station. . . . However, after the party had left for the Capitol, all these plans were delayed. It was really distressing for a while. Nothing ever more resembled a household from which a funeral had just departed with the corpse. Mrs. Taft wandered around the second floor hardly knowing what to do with herself and finally settled at her desk to finish the two letters to her sons. In the meantime one of the ushers turned over the house register to her for final keeping, calling her attention to the fact that a similar book had been presented to Mrs. Cleveland when she left here after the first administration and that, when she brought it back at the beginning of the second term, it formed a connecting link between the two. This suggestion of a possible return of the Taft family brought a real smile to her sad and forlorn face. Then with a parting good-bye the usher left to be about his duties in arranging for the incoming administration. In the meantime Mrs. Taft had changed the hour of her departure from eleven to eleven-thirty. There is no doubt that her regrets at leaving were many, for with all her worries and trials, she had reveled in the life she had lived for the past four years.

Miss Helen having left, everyone just waited for Mrs. Taft to depart. No one cared to go ahead with any visible preparation for the incoming people while she still remained around. An automobile had been in readiness for a half-hour; in fact everyone had merely been standing around waiting for the end so as to prepare again for the beginning. Finally at eleven-thirty Mrs. Taft arose from her desk, put on her hat and furs, and came down on the elevator for the final parting. She had the two letters for her boys and several numbers of recent magazines in her hands and also a large bunch of orchids that had been presented to her earlier in the morning. . . . She was visibly affected when she came into the Usher's Room. In the effort to hand me the two letters, she dropped all the magazines. Everyone who witnessed this last effort was moved to sympathy. Her feelings were so evident that practically no one even attempted to say good-bye to her.

Back in the house everything was as dead as the traditional doornail. For a time there was no mistress, no one to give or approve necessary orders. . . .

It was just two-fifteen when the guests began to arrive. The first comers were strangers to the doorkeepers; a face here and there would be known, but they were as a rule an entirely new lot of people. Finally Mrs. Wilson and her daughters arrived and were shown to the second floor of the house where they were to spend many of their future days and nights. They seemed bewildered, but in a happy frame of mind. They had some meager knowledge of the surroundings from a plan of the house that had been taken to them at Princeton. From this the girls had evidently decided what rooms they were to occupy. They immediately proceeded to locate these rooms, but found them very different from what they had pictured. They marveled at the size of the apartments and only acknowledged that they felt lost. . . .

Mrs. Wilson and her daughters had been upstairs but a short time when they were asked to proceed to the lower floor and join the guests in the East Room. It had been planned beforehand that those assembled should proceed to the dining-room and begin the lunch in advance of the arrival of the party from the Capitol. This after many difficulties was done. It was a hard matter to get the presiding lady and her daughters to go to the dining-room, for they rather hesitated to take the initiative in this, their first social function in their new home. Finally the sound of music told of the approach of the parade and returning party and, in sheer desperation, I exerted strong persuasion on the ladies. They were escorted to the State Dining-Room by the various aides who had returned from the Capitol.

This was just about accomplished when the carriage containing the new President and the ex-President drove under the porte-cochère. Both men alighted from the carriage very quickly. . . . They were both plainly embarrassed, now that they were free from the clamor and shouts of the multitude. President Wilson seemed much more composed than the ex-President, but neither seeming to know just what should be the next move. Presently one of the ushers approached and informed Mr. Wilson that the luncheon party had already assembled in the dining-room. The new President, taking the hint, gallantly turned to Mr. Taft and invited him to join him at lunch. . . . Mr. Taft's Secretary . . . suggested that there was not time for the ex-President to lunch at the White House, as his train left at three-ten and he had to call for Mrs. Taft. . . .

I have no doubt that Mr. Wilson expected Mr. Taft to decline his invitation, for he looked ready to say good-bye. On the contrary, however, Mr. Taft was determined to have that lunch, and . . . replied that surely there was time enough for him to eat a sandwich anyhow. And the way he said it! No one who heard it but whose sympathy was excited. He said it in such a sad way, as if to convey the idea either that he was actually hungry or else just wanted to eat once more within those portals that had been so dear to him for the four years past. Nothing more was said, but those who were aware of the previous efforts to prevent this very thing choked down a feeling of regret, as the two men proceeded to the dining-room together.

. . . The ladies of the household were scattered throughout the room engaged in conversation with those whom they knew, but when the new President entered all tried to reach him for a handshake. It was really sad to observe Mr. Taft. No one seemed to pay any attention to him. It was now necessary for him to do a little hustling for himself, but he managed somehow to get hold of a bit of salad and a sandwich. Word finally came that Mrs. Taft would not wait for him any longer, but would continue on to the station. This was not told to Mr. Taft, but instead he was again reminded that the time was so short he would not have time to go by for Mrs. Taft and to the station unless he left at once. This had the desired effect and he was practically dragged away from the scene of his former achievements.

IRWIN HOOD HOOVER
Forty-Two Years in the White House, 1934

REGENCY TO INTERREGNUM

Woodrow Wilson's family faced far more tragedy than had the Tafts during their eight years in the White House. The President's first wife died in 1914 and, after leading the nation in World War I, Wilson himself fell victim to a stroke. The second Mrs. Wilson recalled the nightmare that began for her on their return from her husband's tour on behalf of the League of Nations — a nightmare that would continue for the last eighteen months of his Presidency.

At eleven on Sunday morning, September 28, 1919, the train pulled its heavy way into Washington, forty-eight hours and seventeen hundred miles from Wichita. A great crowd filled the station and the plaza outside. Margaret [Wilson McAdoo] and the motors were waiting and we were soon back in the blessed shelter of the White House. I was rather unstrung. All those people at the station — my first impulse was to escape them, to get away from what I regarded as prying, curious eyes, though I now realize that the gathering was a sympathetic one.

All the rest of that day my husband wandered like a ghost between the study at one end of the hall and my room at the other. The awful pain in his head that drove him restlessly back and forth was too acute to permit work, or even reading. Late in the afternoon we went for a short motor ride; but still the demon of pain pursued him. . . .

[The third day] since our return, the President seemed a little better. We went for a short ride, and I arranged for the showing of a motion picture in the East Room that evening. Everything went off so well that Woodrow insisted he would read me a chapter from the Bible before retiring, as he had done every night during the War.

He stood under the centre light in my room with the Book in one hand and the other resting on a table that flanked the big couch where I sat. His voice was as vibrant and as strong as I had ever heard it. . . .

I had been sleeping fitfully, getting up every hour or so to see how my husband was. It was so on this night. At five or six in the morning I found him still sleeping normally, as it appeared. Relieved, I dozed off again until after eight. This time I found him sitting on the side of the bed trying to reach a water bottle. As I handed it to him I noticed that his left hand hung loosely. "I have no feeling in that hand," he said. "Will you rub it? But first help me to the bathroom."

He moved with great difficulty, and every move brought spasms of pain; but with my help he gained the bathroom. This so alarmed me that I asked if I could leave him long enough to telephone the Doctor. He said yes, and hurrying into my room I reached Dr. Grayson at his house. While at the 'phone I heard a slight noise, and rushing into my husband's apartment found him on the bathroom floor unconscious.

My first thought was to keep him warm. From his bed I snatched a blanket, and while I was arranging it over him he stirred and asked for a drink of water. I got it, and also got a pillow for his head. . . .

Then came a knock on the door. It was locked; the President and I always locked our doors leading into the hall, leaving only our communicating door unlocked. The knock was Grayson's.

We lifted the President into his bed. He had suffered a stroke, paralyzing the left side of his body. An arm and one leg were useless, but, thank God, the brain was clear and untouched. . . .

Nurses came and the house was organized as a hospital. . . . For days life

The campaign buttons at left represent Benjamin Harrison and Levi P. Morton (center), running mates in the 1888 election; Alton B. Parker and H. G. Davis (top), the Democratic candidates in 1904; their opponents, Theodore Roosevelt and Charles W. Fairbanks (bottom). Above is another T.R. button.

hung in the balance. Then the will to live, to recover and fight on for his League of Nations, almost imperceptibly at first, began to gain ascendency over the forces of disease, and the President got a little better.

Once my husband was out of immediate danger, the burning question was how Mr. Wilson might best serve the country, preserve his own life and if possible recover. Many people, among them some I had counted as friends, have written of my overwhelming ambition to act as President; of my exclusion of all advice, and so forth. I am trying here to write as though I had taken the oath to tell the truth, the whole truth, and nothing but the truth — so help me God.

I asked the doctors to be frank with me; that I must know what the outcome would probably be, so as to be honest with the people. They all said that as the brain was as clear as ever, with the progress made in the past few days, there was every reason to think recovery possible. . . .

But recovery could not be hoped for, they said, unless the President were released from every disturbing problem during these days of Nature's effort to repair the damage done.

"How can that be," I asked the doctors, "when everything that comes to an Executive is a problem? How can I protect him from problems when the country looks to the President as the leader?"

Dr. Dercum leaned towards me and said: "Madam, it is a grave situation, but I think you can solve it. Have everything come to you; weigh the importance of each matter, and see if it is possible by consultations with the respective heads of the Departments to solve them without the guidance of your husband. In this way you can save him a great deal. But always keep in mind that every time you take him a new anxiety or problem to excite him, you are turning a knife in an open wound. His nerves are crying out for rest, and any excitement is torture to him."

"Then," I said, "had he better not resign, let Mr. Marshall succeed to the Presidency and he himself get that complete rest that is so vital to his life?"

"No," the Doctor said, "not if you feel equal to what I suggested. For Mr. Wilson to resign would have a bad effect on the country, and a serious effect on our patient. . . . If he resigns, the greatest incentive to recovery is gone; and as his mind is clear as crystal he can still do more with even a maimed body than any one else. He has the utmost confidence in you. Dr. Grayson tells me he has always discussed public affairs with you; so you will not come to them uninformed."

So began my stewardship. I studied every paper, sent from the different Secretaries or Senators, and tried to digest and present in tabloid form the things that, despite my vigilance, had to go to the President. I, myself, never made a single decision regarding the disposition of public affairs. The only decision that was mine was what was important and what was not, and the very important decision of when to present matters to my husband. . . .

. . . After the Treaty vote in November some little incident with Mexico developed. Senator Albert B. Fall engineered a manoeuvre in the Committee by which a subcommittee was named ostensibly to confer with the President on the Mexican situation. The real object was to see whether the President was mentally capable of administering his office. The subcommittee was composed of Mr. Fall and Mr. Hitchcock. Senator Hitchcock had opposed the whole business, but he consented to accompany Mr. Fall to the White House. When this intelligence was received, the President appointed the morning of the following day to meet the subcommittee.

Senator Fall entered the room looking like a regular Uriah Heap, "washing his hands with invisible soap in imperceptible water." He said to my husband: "Well, Mr. President, we have all been praying for you." "Which way, Senator?" inquired the President with a chuckle. Mr. Fall laughed as if the witticism had been his own.

I had taken the precaution to carry a pad and pencil so I would not have to shake hands with him. I sat on the other side of the bed and carefully wrote down every word that passed between them. Finally, Senator Fall said: "You seem very much engaged, madam." "Yes," I said, "I thought it wise to record this interview so there may be no misunderstanding or misstatements made."

When the Senators rose to leave, Mr. Fall was fulsome in his adieux. Reaching the front door he assured the reporters that the President was mentally fit and had waved both arms in talking and that he had the use of the left as well as his right side which, of course, was an overstatement of the case for Mr. Wilson's left side was nearly useless.

EDITH G. WILSON
My Memoir, 1939

The Republican presidents who occupied the White House in the 1920's could not compete with Wilson's leadership or brilliance, but the nation seemed content with lesser men. "Silent Cal" Coolidge and his vivacious wife, Grace, inspired one bright moment in the history of White House literature when they invited humorist Will Rogers to be their guest in October 1926.

Now there was the President of a Country a third as big as Russia and more than half as big as China. He and the Leading Lady of our land, waiting dinner on a Lowbrow Comedian. Now if any Nation can offer any more of a demonstration of Democracy than that, I would like to hear of it. . . .

Mr. Coolidge met me very cordially. He was accompanied by another gentleman that I couldent see well enough to recognize. He was called "The White House Spokesman." Now if you don't know what one of those are, I will tell you. Well he is some friend of the President's that Mr. Coolidge conceived the idea of sorter having around handy in case he wanted to say anything for publication; or in case he said anything that was not for publication, why it is better to let it be said by The White House Spokesman. You see Mr. Coolidge don't say much anyway himself, and for publication he don't say anything. . . .

Mind you, nothing is getting by him. He is taking in everything, but he ain't just what you would call bubbling over. A joke don't excite him any more than a Republican Senatorial defeat. He takes everything sorter docile. But with it all he is mighty friendly and nice, and talks a whole lot when he is with somebody that he feels can't tell him anything. . . .

We are sitting there at the table, just the three of us, chatting away about a little of everything, and here is something I want any of you children to know: If you have a dog and your mother won't let you feed it at the table, . . . go right on and feed your dog, Kids; it's being done in one of our best homes.

The Coolidges have a couple of flea hounds and they was handing out

In 1908 a vote for the Republican candidates, William H. Taft and James S. Sherman, was a vote for prosperity. Such, at least, seems to be the message that this Uncle Sam hat bank was intended to convey.

things to them all the time. One of them would come to Mr. Coolidge's place and one to hers, and they seemed to think an awful lot of them two dogs, and the dogs certainly were crazy about them. Well, they was feeding the Dogs so much that at one time it looked to me like the dogs was getting more than I was.

. . . [The] Butler was so slow bringing one course that I come pretty near getting down on my all fours and barking to see if business wouldent pick up with me. . . .

We had fish that night for dinner. Well, I never paid much attention to the fish. I paid enough attention to it to eat it, but I never gave it any more thought. . . .

[But the next day at lunch] the Butler come to Mr. Coolidge with a platter of something that resembled some kind of hash. The White House spokesman looked at it and asked, "Same old fish?" Well, that sure did sound homelike. I had forgot about the fish the night before, but he hadent. To hear the family discussing the rehash brought me right back among the mortals. I had eaten Turkey hash for generally about a week after holidays and Weddings. Chicken hash generally runs about two days. I had partaken of Beef hash, and I have eaten hash that nobody knows what the contents were. But when you get down to eating fish hash you are flirting with Economy.

WILL ROGERS
*A Letter from a Self-Made Diplomat
to his Constituents,* 1927

One of the most painfully embarrassing moments in White House history occurred seven years later when the Republicans surrendered the Executive Mansion to its first Democratic tenant since 1921. The depression had turned the nation's political allegiance, and Franklin D. Roosevelt had easily defeated Herbert Hoover in November 1932. Roosevelt's son James accompanied his parents to the White House for an awkward meeting with the Hoovers.

On March 3, 1933, the day before he was to take office as President of the United States, Father asked me to accompany Mother and him to the White House for their preinaugural protocol call on President and Mrs. Hoover. He did this for two reasons: First, he had a strong sense of history which he liked to share, when possible, with his children, and, second, he needed help in walking and preferred on this particular occasion to be assisted by a member of his family.

It would be putting it mildly to state that Mr. Hoover was not happy with Father. It was obvious that he had taken his defeat as even more of a personal humiliation than it should have been.

In any event, in the lame duck months between Mr. Hoover's defeat and Father's inauguration, the country's economic plight grew worse, and the outgoing President made repeated attempts . . . to involve Father in sharing the responsibilities — on Mr. Hoover's terms. Father . . . would have cooperated with any acceptable measures for the good of the country. He had no intention, however, of letting Mr. Hoover maneuver him into a position in which he would share the blame for the retiring Chief Executive's repudiated policies. So, politely but skillfully, Father dodged every time the

One of Woodrow Wilson's 1916 campaign slogans, "The world must be made safe for democracy," is printed beneath his portrait on the election bandana above. The 1920 campaign toy at right was operated by a lever that made it seem as if the cut-out image of the Republican candidate, Warren G. Harding, was thumbing its nose — presumably at Harding's opponent, James M. Cox.

gloomy Mr. Hoover sought to lasso him.

All this did not tend to create a congenial atmosphere on the afternoon Father, Mother, my wife, and I paid our courtesy call to the Pennsylvania Avenue mansion which was to be Father's and Mother's home for more years than they anticipated. The call was made at tea time, and we were to be received in the Green Room. . . . In a short while, Mrs. Hoover appeared. She was extremely gracious, a thorough-going lady.

Then we sat. To the best of my recollection, fully thirty minutes went by. It seemed even longer. Father was imperturbable and betrayed no irritation. I kept looking at him and could see, however, that he did not like it.

At last President Hoover entered. To Father's astonishment, for no hint had been given that this would be anything but a social call, he was accompanied by the outgoing Secretary of the Treasury, the late Ogden Mills, Father's conservative Dutchess County neighbor and one of the principal architects of the fiscal policies to which Father did not intend to be pinned. . . .

I sat there fascinated as Father gave me one of my earliest lessons in how to avoid political booby traps. As soon as Mr. Hoover made reference to the fact that Secretary Mills had been invited because his presence might be helpful, Father cut in, courteously but firmly, and observed that he certainly would not presume to bring up any serious discussions on this purely social occasion; before he would undertake to discuss any fiscal matters, he said, he would want his own advisers with him.

That pretty much broke up the party. We downed our tea, Mother and Mrs. Hoover made desultory conversation, and then it was time to go.

At this point, Father attempted to make a graceful gesture. "Mr. President," he remarked, "as you know it is rather difficult for me to move in a hurry. It takes me a little while to get up and I know how busy you must be, sir, so please don't wait for me."

Mr. Hoover just stood up, looked at Father bleakly, and said in his low monotone: "Mr. Roosevelt, after you have been President for a while, you will learn that the President of the United States waits for no one." With that, and with no amenities, he strode from the room, Ogden Mills behind him. Mrs. Hoover looked embarrassed; she shook hands all around and then she left, too, leaving the prospective "new tenants" on their own to make their departure.

JAMES ROOSEVELT AND SIDNEY SHALETT
Affectionately, F.D.R., 1959

CAMELOT AND AFTER

While all presidential families are the object of public curiosity, perhaps none fascinated Americans as much as did the Kennedys. Every item in the daily life of John and Jacqueline Kennedy and their two young children was reported by the press and eagerly studied by the reading public. Arthur Schlesinger, Jr., the distinguished historian who served as a Kennedy aide, offered this view of family life at the White House with a special insight into the personality of a First Lady whose charm and beauty sometimes obscured her intelligence and efficiency.

The day began at quarter to eight. George Thomas, his devoted and humorous Negro valet, would knock at the door of the Kennedy bedroom. As he sat down before his breakfast tray, surrounded by the morning papers and urgent cables and reports which may have come in during the night, Caroline and John would rush in, greet their father and turn on the television to watch animated cartoons. Then more presidential reading, with the television going full blast. At nine o'clock a calisthenics program came on, and Kennedy liked to watch the children tumble on the bedroom floor in rhythm with the man on the screen. Then, taking one of the children by the hand, he would walk over to the presidential office in the West Wing.

After a morning of work and a swim, often with David Powers, in the White House pool, he returned to the Mansion for luncheon. He preferred to lunch alone or with Jacqueline; very occasionally he brought guests. After luncheon came the nap. Impressed by Churchill's eloquence in praise of afternoon rest, he had begun this practice in the Senate. It was a genuine sleep, in pajamas and under covers. He went off at once; and in forty-five minutes would awaken and chat as he dressed. This was Jacqueline's hour of the day, as the morning was the children's.

This historian, it must be said, had not realized how constricted the living quarters of an American President were. The first floor of the Mansion was given over to public rooms and reserved for state occasions. The third floor was rarely mentioned. The private life of the Kennedys took place on the second floor under conditions which an average Park Avenue tycoon would regard as claustrophobic. A long dark corridor, brightened by a set of Catlin's Indian paintings, transected the floor. Bedrooms debouched from each side. A yellow oval room, marvelously light and lovely, was used for tea or drinks before dinner; it had served earlier Presidents as an office. Another room at the west end of the corridor was Jacqueline's room by day and the sitting room in the evening. Dinner guests resorted to the President's own bathroom. It was not a house for spacious living. Yet, until Theodore Roosevelt persuaded the Congress to build the West Wing, Presidents not only raised their families in these crowded quarters but ran the country from them.

It never seemed unduly crowded in these days. The atmosphere was always one of informality. When his family was away, the President used to have his afternoon appointments on the second floor. But generally he returned to the West Wing after his nap, where he worked until seven-thirty or eight at night. Jacqueline liked to guard the evenings for relaxation, and the President welcomed the relief from the incessant business of the day. . . .

After the first year, they left the White House very seldom for private dinners elsewhere. . . . Instead, Jacqueline would arrange small dinners of six, eight or ten in the Mansion. They were informal and gay, the most agreeable occasions in the world. One memorable evening celebrated Stravinsky's seventy-fifth birthday. The composer, who had been rehearsing all day, was both excited and tired. A Chicago newspaper publisher, also present, insisted on talking across him at dinner to the President about such issues as Katanga and Medicare. Stravinsky said to me later, "They were speaking about matters which I did not understand and about which I did not care. I became an alien in their midst." But then the President toasted him and Stravinsky, obviously moved, responded with immense charm. On less formal evenings Jacqueline would sometimes put on phonograph records and there might be a moment of dancing. The President often vanished silently into his bedroom to work or make phone calls, reappearing in time to bid his guests goodnight. Occasionally there were films in the projection room in the

East Wing. Kennedy was not a great movie fan and tended, unless the film was unusually gripping, to walk out after the first twenty or thirty minutes. . . .

The state dinners were inevitable, but Jacqueline made them bearable by ending the old regimented formality of solemn receiving lines and stilted conversation and changing them into elegant and cheerful parties, beautifully mingling informality and dignity. When asked about White House dinners, people would now say with surprise that they really had a very good time. But the gala occasions were the small dinner dances. Jacqueline conceived them as a means of restoring a larger social gaiety to her husband's life. . . . There were not many such parties — only five in the whole time in the White House — and they were all blithe and enchanting evenings. The President seemed renewed by them and walked with a springier step the next day. . . .

The White House was temporary for the Kennedys but permanent for the nation. Mrs. Eisenhower had taken her successor on a trip around the Mansion in November 1960. . . . [Mrs. Kennedy] trudged through the historic rooms, long since emptied of the authentic past, now filled with mediocre reproductions; it seemed almost as if this were a house in which nothing had ever taken place. She resolved on the spot to establish the President's residence thereafter as unequivocally the nation's house and transform it into a house of which the nation could be thoroughly proud. . . .

Her hope was to recover as many as possible of the old and beautiful objects which past Presidents had cherished and make the President's house both a distillation of American history and an expression of American excellence. "Everything in the White House must have a reason for being there," she said. "It would be sacrilege merely to 'redecorate' it — a word I hate. It must be restored — and that has nothing to do with decoration. That is a question of scholarship." Her husband sent Clark Clifford to help with her plans. But Clifford, remembering the furor over the innocuous balcony Truman had added to the south portico, was dubious; "you just can't make any changes in the White House," he said. Jacqueline, however, soon talked him around and with his help set up the White House Historical Association. She enlisted Henry du Pont, James Fosburgh and others on a Committee of the Fine Arts Commission for the White House and procured legislation designating the White House as a museum and enabling it to receive gifts. The restoration program went speedily ahead. Exploring the White House basement herself, she uncovered a superbly carved desk made of oak timbers from a British frigate and installed it in the presidential office in the West Wing. Soon she pushed through the publication of the first White House guidebook in the nation's history. It was a formidable executive effort, but she carried it out with a perfectionist's attention to detail, steely determination and lovely command. The President gave her his full support, applauded as the inherited furniture was carted away and watched the transformation with mounting pride. . . . He congratulated her as the number of people going through the White House steadily rose: in 1962 the total was nearly two-thirds greater than in 1960. In February 1962, when Mrs. Kennedy took the whole nation on a television tour of the new White House, the President viewed the program with great satisfaction.

ARTHUR M. SCHLESINGER, JR.
A Thousand Days, 1965

The shadow of John Kennedy's assassination darkened the first months of Lyndon Johnson's administration, and growing national disunity over the war in Southeast Asia shaped the end of his term in office. Lady Bird Johnson's diary carried this account of March 31, 1968 — the day when her husband announced that he would not seek reelection.

When I went back into Lyndon's room, his face was sagging and there was such pain in his eyes as I had not seen since his mother died. But he didn't have time for grief. Today was a crescendo of a day. At 9 in the evening, Lyndon was to make his talk to the nation about the war. The speech was not yet firm. There were still revisions to be made and people to see. . . .

. . . It was a day of coming and going — and it's hard to remember when what happened. Sometime during the morning Buzz [White House aide Horace Busby] came in, took up his place in the Treaty Room, and began to work on the speech. I had spent a good part of Saturday and part of Friday making suggestions on it myself. I read it over again for what was the umpteenth time, and then . . . Lyndon said to [our friends] Arthur and Mathilde Krim and me, "What do you think about this? This is what I'm going to put at the end of the speech." And he read a very beautifully written statement which ended, "Accordingly, I shall not seek and I will not accept the nomination of my party for another term as your President."

The four of us had talked about this over and over, and hour after hour, but somehow we all acted and felt stunned. Maybe it was the calm finality in Lyndon's voice, and maybe we believed him for the first time. Arthur said something like, "You can't mean this!" And Mathilde exclaimed in an excited way, "Oh no, no!" Then we all began to discuss the reasons why, and why not, over and over again.

. . . Finally, a little after 2 o'clock Lyndon and I, and Luci and Pat, and Mathilde and Arthur went to the table for lunch. . . .

Mathilde's eyes were full of tears, and Luci had obviously been crying forthrightly. Lyndon seemed to be congealing into a calm, quiet state of mind, out of our reach. And I, what did I feel? . . . so uncertain of the future that I would not dare to try to persuade him one way or the other. There was much in me that cried out to go on, to call on every friend we have, to give and work, to spend and fight, right up to the last. And if we lost, well and good — we were free! But if we didn't run, we could be free without all this draining of our friends. I think what was uppermost — what was going over and over in Lyndon's mind — was what I've heard him say increasingly these last months: "I do not believe I can unite this country". . . .

Sometime during the afternoon . . . Lyndon went to his office, and I talked to Lynda and to Luci. Both of them were emotional, crying and distraught. What does this do to the servicemen? They will think — What have I been sent out here for? . . .

Later in the afternoon, I talked to Lyndon about what the girls had said. He said, "I called in General Westmoreland last year about that, about how it would affect the morale of the men. He thinks it will not matter appreciably". . . . He looked at me rather distantly and said, "I think General Westmoreland knows more about it than they [the girls] do". . . .

It was a strange afternoon and evening. We would meet in the West Hall by twos or threes, or all of us . . . and look at each other, helplessly, silent,

An elephant and a donkey, symbols of the Republican and the Democratic parties, bang the political drum in the wind-up toy above, a souvenir of the 1952 presidential campaign. Another memento of that election is a Republican "clean-up" bucket (below), which was directed at alleged Democratic corruption.

or exploding with talk. I felt as if I ought to do *something*. I must *do* something — but what? . . . I remember that I kept on looking at the hands of the clock, and counting the hours until 9 P.M. and the broadcast. . . .

I went over with Clark [Clifford] and Buzz a few minutes before 9 and Lynda joined us. And there we were in the familiar oval office of the President, the floor a jungle of cables, under the brilliant glare of TV lights. What a stage setting!

Lyndon, very quiet, sat at his desk. The lines in his face were deep, but there was a marvelous sort of repose over-all. And the seconds ticked away.

I went to him and said quietly, "Remember — pacing and drama." It was a great speech and I wanted him to get the greatest out of it — and I did not know what the end would be.

The speech was magnificently delivered. He's best, I think, in the worst of times, calm and strong — those who love him must have loved him more. And those who hate him must at least have thought: "Here is a man."

Then came the end of the speech. . . .

"I do not believe that I should devote an hour or a day of my time to any personal partisan causes or to any duties other than the awesome duties of this office — the Presidency of your country. Accordingly, I shall not seek, and I will not accept, the nomination of my party for another term as your President."

Lynda and I had been sitting down, behind us Luci and Pat standing. Luci threw her arms around Lyndon. She was obviously holding back the tears, but just barely. Lynda kissed him, and Pat shook hands.

Then there was a great blur of confusion, and we walked out of the President's office and went back to the second floor. . . .

. . . Nearly everybody just looked staggered and struck silent — and then the phones began to ring.

. . . I was called to the phone by Abigail [Mrs. Eugene] McCarthy, who said, "Bird, Bird, you know what I've always thought of you." And then she said, "When he made the announcement, I could only think of you standing in front of the Wilson portrait . . ." And she didn't have to go on. I know what I always think in front of the Wilson portrait. In that face you see the toll the office and the times extracted. Its message to me is: "A President should have his portrait painted reasonably early in the office."

LADY BIRD JOHNSON
A White House Diary, 1970

A DUKE IN THE WHITE HOUSE

Before his inauguration in 1969, Richard Nixon had been known as a reserved and serious man seldom given to gaiety and humor. However, observers sensed something different in the new President. In April 1969 Edward "Duke" Ellington was honored by a White House birthday party at which he received the Presidential Medal of Freedom. A Newsweek *writer gave this first-hand account.*

At an after-dinner toast the President noted that Ellington's father had once served in the same room at state dinners as a butler in the White House . . . and said: "I, and many others here, have been guests at state dinners. I have been here when an emperor has been toasted. I have been here when we have raised our glasses to a king, to presidents, and to prime ministers. But in studying the history of all the great dinners held in this room, never before has a duke been toasted. Let's raise our glasses to the greatest duke of them all. Duke Ellington."

Then the soul party started. Before a packed audience in the East Room, President Nixon, in a light mood, presented Ellington with the Presidential Medal of Freedom. . . . He pretended to do a double take in noticing the Duke's full name: "I was looking at this name on here. It says 'Edward Kennedy Ellington' ". . . . Then, in a more serious tone, he read the citation. . . .

Before replying, the Duke planted four kisses on the President's cheek, and the Duke's musician friends roared with laughter. The light mood of the evening was set. The President moved toward the piano with a "Ladies and gentlemen, please don't go away . . . one number is missing on the program . . . please stand and sing, and please, in the key of G. 'Happy Birthday.' "

Then the virtuoso concert began, a serenade to the Duke by the all-star band playing an especially arranged program of Duke Ellington music. . . . The musicians vied with one another to come up with new and exciting arrangements. . . . The usual White House entertainment lasts 30 minutes; the jazz group was first given 45 minutes, which after rehearsal was pushed to one hour. The musicians were told, by Willis Conover, to play it by ear and watch the audience response. The musicians did, and stopped playing after an estimated one hour and a half.

After the concert, at the President's suggestion that "we ought to hear from the Duke too," Ellington improvised a number — "something graceful and gentle" — that he dedicated to "Pat."

Then the President, with a "Ladies and gentlemen, the evening is still young" retired with the First Lady to the private living quarters. Upstairs, he told a friend: "It was the best evening I can remember." He went to bed but it is doubtful that he went to sleep.

Downstairs, the guests were moved . . . out of the East Room temporarily and into the east hall and adjoining rooms. Shortly after . . . the Marine Band marched into the East Room playing "The Saints Go Marching In," a social ploy to get the guests moving back into the East Room for the jam session. . . .

. . . At first some of the guests sat in the chairs and listened. The President's secretary Rosemary Woods did a few dance turns by herself in an empty space behind the chairs. Then a few dancers took courage. And soon, the small area between the bandstand and the chairs took on the look of a small discotheque. . . .

The hot jazz session went on and on and ended sometime after 2 A.M. It led Mrs. Arthur Logan, whose husband is Ellington's doctor in New York . . . to say: "If this thing doesn't break up soon I'm going to head for the Lincoln Bedroom." Said a waiter: "I've never seen the house like this. It sure has soul tonight."

JANE WHITMORE
Newsweek, 1969

The sprightly Kennedy campaign hat above and the Nixon banner below were used in the 1960 battle between the two for the Presidency.

REFERENCE

Chronology of American History

Entries in boldface refer to the White House.

1775	Battles of Lexington and Concord mark the beginning of the American Revolution
1776	Declaration of Independence adopted by Continental Congress
1777	Articles of Confederation ratified
1783	Treaty of Paris acknowledges U.S. independence
1787	Constitutional Convention held at Philadelphia
1788	Constitution ratified
1789	George Washington inaugurated first President; Bill of Rights confirmed
1790	Congress passes Residence Bill authorizing selection of land for permanent capital on Potomac River; capital moved from New York to Philadelphia
1791	Washington selects acreage for capital; appoints L'Enfant to plan Federal District; **Washington and L'Enfant make final selection of site for President's House**
1792	**American architect James Hoban wins competition for design of presidential home**
1794	Federal troops put down Whiskey Rebellion
1798	Alien and Sedition acts passed by Congress
1799	**Construction of White House frame completed**
1800	Government officially moves to Washington, D.C.; **President John Adams and his wife, Abigail, move into the White House**
1801–9	**President Thomas Jefferson supervises completion of White House; Benjamin H. Latrobe serves as architect**
1803	Louisiana Purchase; *Marbury* v. *Madison* establishes the principle of judicial review
1804	Lewis and Clark expedition
1807	**Pavilions and terraces, designed by President Jefferson, added to White House**
1809	**Congress authorizes $26,000 for White House repairs and refurnishing**
1812–14	War of 1812
1814	**British burn White House and other buildings in the capital**
1816	**James Hoban begins work to restore White House**
1817	**President James Monroe moves into reconstructed White House**

1820	Missouri Compromise temporarily resolves slavery question in new territories; **Maria Hester Monroe weds Samuel L. Gouverneur, first wedding ceremony held in the White House**
1823	Monroe Doctrine promulgated
1824	**South Portico constructed**
1825	Erie Canal opened
1829–37	Administration of Andrew Jackson nationalizes the "spoils system," increasing power of political parties
1829	**North Portico built**
1841	William Henry Harrison dies after one month in office, succeeded by John Tyler
1845	Annexation of Texas
1846	Oregon treaty establishes northwestern boundary
1846–48	War with Mexico
1848	Mexican cession adds territories of New Mexico and California; discovery of gold in California; first Women's Rights Convention held in Seneca Falls, New York
1850	Compromise of 1850 attempts to settle increasingly bitter sectional dispute; Millard Fillmore succeeds Zachary Taylor; **White House library begun by Abigail Fillmore**
1852	Publication of Harriet Beecher Stowe's novel, *Uncle Tom's Cabin*
1854	Kansas-Nebraska Act allows new states to decide slavery question by popular vote
1856	Republican Party runs first presidential candidate
1857	*Dred Scott* decision denies civil liberties to slaves
1860	**Arrival of Japanese ambassador marks first White House visit by Orientals;** Abraham Lincoln elected President; South Carolina leads secession of southern states
1861	Civil War begins with fall of Fort Sumter; **soldiers quartered in the East Room of the White House**
1861–62	**Mary Lincoln undertakes extensive refurbishing of White House**
1863	**Emancipation Proclamation signed by President Lincoln in his Cabinet room;** first national conscription order passed by Congress; riots against conscription occur in many cities

1865	General Robert E. Lee surrenders to General Ulysses S. Grant at Appomattox Court House; President Lincoln assassinated; Andrew Johnson becomes President; ratification of Thirteenth Amendment abolishes slavery
1867	Secretary of State William Seward negotiates purchase of Alaska from Russia for $7,200,000
1868	Ratification of Fourteenth Amendment guarantees civil rights to Negroes; President Johnson impeached by House, acquitted in Senate by one vote
1869	Completion of Union Pacific, first transcontinental railroad
1872–73	Crédit Mobilier scandal
1873	**Structural repairs and redecoration of White House during Grant administration**
1876	Rutherford B. Hayes elected President in disputed contest
1877	**Lucy Hayes holds first Easter egg-rolling contest on White House lawn**
1881	James A. Garfield assassinated; succeeded by Chester A. Arthur; **President Arthur redecorates White House**
1883	Pendleton Act establishes civil service system
1886	**President Grover Cleveland marries Frances Folsom in the Blue Room — first, and only, President to be married in the White House;** American Federation of Labor organized
1887	Interstate Commerce Commission established
1889	**Caroline Harrison begins White House china collection;** opening of Oklahoma territory for settlement
1890	Sherman Anti-Trust Act passed
1896	In *Plessy* v. *Ferguson* Supreme Court holds separate but equal facilities constitutional
1898	Spanish-American War
1901	President William A. McKinley assassinated; Theodore Roosevelt becomes President
1902	**Modernization and enlargement of White House undertaken by Roosevelt; West Wing added**
1909	**President's Oval Office built**
1914	World War I begins in Europe; Panama Canal opened

1917	United States enters World War I
1918	Armistice signed ending World War I
1920	Ratification of Nineteenth Amendment provides women's suffrage
1923–24	Calvin Coolidge succeeds Warren Harding; Teapot Dome scandal
1923–28	**Grace Coolidge begins restoration of historical antiques to White House; enlargement of the Executive Mansion's third floor**
1929	**Fire damages executive office wing;** stock market crash marks beginning of Great Depression
1933–36	Period of New Deal legislation to aid economic recovery
1939	World War II begins in Europe
1941	Japan attacks Pearl Harbor; U.S. enters World War II
1942	**Building of East Wing**
1945	President Franklin D. Roosevelt dies; Harry S. Truman succeeds; World War II ends
1948	Congress authorizes Marshall Plan to spur European economic recovery
1948–52	**Major renovation and enlargement of White House under Truman**
1949	Senate ratifies NATO treaty
1950–52	Korean conflict
1954	Supreme Court's decision in *Brown* v. *Board of Education* holds that public school segregation is unconstitutional
1959	Alaska and Hawaii admitted to union
1961–63	**Jacqueline Kennedy begins major restoration of White House furnishings, acquiring many historic antiques**
1963	President John F. Kennedy assassinated; Lyndon B. Johnson becomes President
1964	Civil Rights Law passed; **President Johnson establishes Commission for Preservation of the White House — provides for permanent office of Curator**
1968	Voting Rights Act passed
1969	American astronauts first men to land on the moon
1971–72	**Refurbishing of public rooms in White House undertaken by Patricia Nixon**

Guide to the White House

The White House is both a private residence and a public institution. As the home of the presidents of the United States during their terms of office, it has been the scene of joyous and tragic family events—of births, weddings, deaths; as the seat of the executive branch of government, it has been at the hub of historic political decisions—affecting the nation and the world. With varying degrees of success, each succeeding First Family has had to cope with this duality.

When the first residents, John and Abigail Adams, moved into the still-unfinished White House in November 1800, they found its size more than adequate. By the middle of the nineteenth century, however, the increasing demands upon the Presidency had created severe overcrowding. But with the expansions and renovations of the twentieth century—particularly the removal of the offices of the President and his staff to newly constructed wings and the opening of state rooms on the ground floor—the space limitations appear to have been solved. Today the Executive Mansion is a smoothly run, efficient organization with a household staff of 70, capable of entertaining as many as 2,000 guests for official dinners and receptions and of welcoming 1,500,000 tourists a year. (See plan page 166.)

The visitor embarking on a public tour enters the White House through a special entrance in the East Wing, decorated with portraits of Franklin D. Roosevelt, Woodrow Wilson, John Tyler, and William H. Taft, among others. The extension, built during the administration of Franklin Delano Roosevelt, incorporates Thomas Jefferson's 1807 pavilion. Also in the East Wing but closed to the public are offices for the First Lady's assistants and other members of the White House staff.

Tourists approach the main house along a windowed corridor that overlooks the Jacqueline Kennedy Garden. The upkeep of this beautifully landscaped area is the responsibility of the National Park Service, as is the care of the entire eighteen-acre property that surrounds the Executive Mansion. A changing display of exhibits and memorabilia associated with the Presidency fills the cabinets in this corridor.

As conceived by James Hoban, the Irish architect whose 1792 plan was chosen from among entries that included an anonymous design submitted by Thomas Jefferson, the White House was to be a three-story structure. Financial considerations, however, reduced the completed house to only two stories. The floor the tourist first enters is the former basement of Hoban's White House. But in 1902, Theodore Roosevelt employed the firm of McKim, Mead & White to modernize the building. Among the architects' innovations were the remodeling of those old storage rooms and the creation of an elegant ground floor with its own entrance below the original one on the South Portico.

Although none of the five main rooms on the ground floor is open to the general public, tourists can enjoy the gallery of first ladies' portraits in the arch-vaulted corridor—among them the striking study of Eleanor Roosevelt by Douglas Chandor and the controversial portrait of Jacqueline Kennedy by Aaron Shikler.

Throughout its nearly two-hundred-year history, the White House has been furnished by each presidential family according to its own private tastes.

Rarely was any consideration given to the historic nature of the house or to the preservation of its interior furnishings. In 1882, for instance, Chester A. Arthur auctioned twenty-four wagon-loads of furniture—including pieces that had been in the White House for half a century. Prior to 1962, apart from necessary structural changes, only sporadic attempts were made to undo such cavalier treatment. Finally, under the direction of Jacqueline Kennedy, a new approach was instituted: the White House would henceforth be decorated with fine American and French period furniture and with items associated with past presidents. With the aid of purchases and donations, that policy has been continued by successive administrations.

Few changes have been made in the ground-floor **Library** since 1962. It is decorated in the style of the early nineteenth century. Its pale yellow walls are lined with shelves containing several thousand volumes of fiction and nonfiction by representative American authors.

The furnishings of the Library include a set of caned furniture by Duncan Phyfe, a nineteenth-century New York cabinetmaker. Suspended from the ceiling is a red tole and crystal chandelier from the home of the novelist James Fenimore Cooper; on the walls are portraits by Charles Bird King of five Plains Indians who visited President Monroe in 1821.

Across the corridor, on the southern side of the building, are four interconnected rooms. The first is the **Gold** or **Vermeil Room.** President Truman played billiards in this room; today it serves as a ladies' withdrawing room. On display in glass-enclosed cabinets is a large collection of English and French vermeil pieces. The exquisite cups, trays, tureens, and pitchers, a 1956 bequest to the White House by Mrs. Margaret Thompson Biddle, are valued at more than $1,000,000.

The simple furnishings form an unobtrusive backdrop to the dazzling exhibit. Hanging in the Vermeil Room are a pencil-and-sepia drawing known as *The Apotheosis of Franklin,* by the French artist Jean Honoré Fragonard, painted in commemoration of the American statesman's visit to the Louvre; and Claude Monet's *Morning on the Seine,* donated in memory of John F. Kennedy by his family.

The White House china collection was begun in 1889 by Mrs. Benjamin Harrison. By 1917 it had grown so large that Mrs. Woodrow Wilson set aside a special ground-floor room, the **China Room,** to display the collection. Samples of both state and family dinner services used by past presidents are on display, including Chinese export porcelain, eighteenth-century Sèvres plates, and Lenox and Wedgwood china. A stunning full-length portrait of Grace Coolidge in evening dress, by Howard Chandler Christy, hangs in the China Room.

A distinctive architectural feature of Hoban's plan for the White House was the creation of an oval reception room on the first floor, now known as the Blue Room. Directly below it on the ground floor is a matching oval chamber, the **Diplomatic Reception Room.** Before the renovations of 1902 it was the mansion's boiler room. Franklin Roosevelt broadcast his famous "fireside chats" from this room; today it is furnished as an early nineteenth-century drawing room — with American Sheraton furniture purchased by Mamie Eisenhower — and is the official entrance for the Presi-

dent, his family, and guests on state occasions. A door opens onto the south lawn and the Jefferson and Washington memorials can be seen in the distance.

On the curved walls of the Diplomatic Reception Room is a rare paper, "Scenic America," printed by the French firm Zuber and Co. in 1834. It is a panoramic unfolding of eastern America's natural scenic beauty: Niagara Falls, the Natural Bridge of Virginia, Boston Harbor, West Point, and New York Bay. A blue and gold rug and furniture upholstered in pale gold complement the striking paper.

A door leads from the Diplomatic Reception Room to the **Map Room,** opened in 1970. In F.D.R.'s former "situation room" during World War II, a private conference and sitting room for the President and First Lady has been created. The only room in the White House that features American Chippendale furniture, the Map Room has an historic eighteenth-century map and a splendid collection of contemporary maps. The remaining rooms on the ground floor include the offices of the curator, doctor, and housekeeper, and kitchen facilities.

Tourists ascend a marble staircase to the first floor; five of the six state rooms are open for public viewing. This steady stream of visitors makes frequent refurbishing of the rooms necessary. In 1971 and 1972, for example, the Green, Blue, and Red rooms were substantially redecorated by the Nixons. Architecturally, the first floor appears almost as it was originally designed, although one of two main stairways to the second floor was eliminated in 1902 in order to enlarge the State Dining Room.

The walls and floors of the **Entrance Hall** on the first floor are of marble. A

mirror and a single glorious cut-glass chandelier accentuate the vastness of the space, which is furnished with settees and recent presidential portraits. Four marble pillars separate the Entrance Hall from the long red-carpeted **Cross Hall** that runs the length of the house. Until 1902 an *art nouveau* stained-glass screen by Louis Tiffany, commissioned by President Arthur, separated the two halls. The Cross Hall contains two additional chandeliers similar to the one in the Entrance Hall and other portraits of recent presidents.

Perhaps the most famous room in the White House is the spacious **East Room.** Decorated in classic off-white and gold, and sparsely furnished, the East Room functions as the main salon for official receptions and gala entertainments.

In the elegant East Room is the beloved Gilbert Stuart portrait of **George** Washington, which Dolley Madison rescued at the eleventh hour before the White House was burned by the British in 1814. Beside it is a companion portrait of Martha Washington by E. F. Andrews. Three large chandeliers hang from the twenty-two-foot-high ceiling. At the northern end of the room, the largest in the mansion, is a mahogany Steinway piano with gilded eagle supports. Set against mirrors above the two mantelpieces on the south wall are French bronze-doré candelabra purchased by James Monroe.

Connecting doors lead from the East Room to the Green, Blue, and Red rooms, each furnished with authentic antiques. The **Green Room** is decorated in the Sheraton or American classical style. It has been used as a parlor since the Madison administration. After the 1814 fire, Monroe ordered the room's elaborate marble mantelpiece. With its

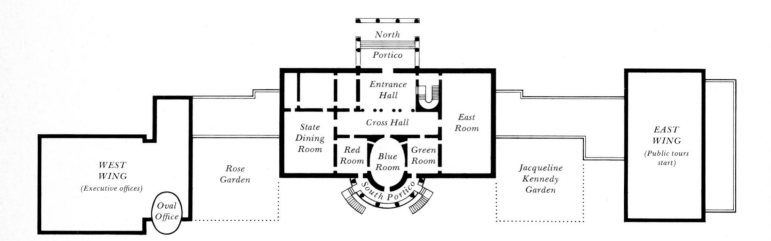

mate, now in the Red Room, it is the only original mantelpiece still in the White House. Monroe reupholstered the furniture in green fabrics and established the traditional color scheme. The walls are covered with green moiréd silk and much of the Sheraton furniture is attributed to Duncan Phyfe. Today the Green Room functions as an informal parlor.

In 1948 President Truman noticed vibrations in the floor of his second-floor study, above the oval Blue Room, the most formal room in the White House. Investigation revealed that the hasty 1902 renovation and the enlargement of the third story in 1927 had dangerously weakened the structure. Over a four-year period the interior of the building was removed and then restored; the original walls were reinforced with a steel framework.

Today the **Blue Room** is furnished much as it was during the tenure of James Monroe. When Monroe moved into the rebuilt White House in 1817, he ordered a new suite of furniture for the room from the French cabinetmaker Pierre Antoine Bellangé. Over the years many of the pieces were dispersed but several have been located and placed again in the Blue Room. The wallpaper, a hand-screened reproduction of an antique Directoire pattern created in France in 1800, is typical of styles that may have adorned the walls of the White House in the first quarter of the nineteenth century. Among the paintings in the room are two of special merit: the famous Rembrandt Peale life study of Thomas Jefferson and a dynamic portrait of John Tyler by George P. A. Healy.

The **Red Room** is an intimate sitting room or parlor in the American Empire style of 1815–20. The walls are hung with brilliant "Dolley Madison" red silk and shades of scarlet red predominate throughout. The antique mahogany furniture includes a superb American sofa with gilded dolphin feet; a sofa, with bronze sphinx heads beneath the armrests; American Empire side chairs and lyre-based card tables; and an unusual circular gueridon table with an inlaid marble top made by Charles Honoré Lannuier, a New York cabinetmaker. Also in the Red Room is a small music stand on which is a copy of "Lafayette's March," composed in honor of the French general's 1824 tour of America. On the mantel are an eighteenth-century French musical clock presented to the White House by President Auriol of France in 1952 and a pair of French gilt porcelain vases decorated with oval paintings of Washington and Lafayette. A marble bust of Martin Van Buren appears in the lovely portrait by Henry Inman of Angelica Van Buren — the President's daughter-in-law and hostess — that hangs over the mantel. The bust itself, carved by Hiram Powers, perches on a pedestal on the south wall of the room. It is the finest example of American sculpture in the White House.

There are two dining rooms on the first floor. The large **State Dining Room,** repaneled in 1902 in a classical style, can accommodate approximately 130 guests for formal dinners. Most of the furnishings of the gold and white room date from Theodore Roosevelt's renovation: the chandelier and wall sconces, the set of high-backed Queen Anne chairs (reproductions), and the three consoles with gilded eagle supports. The chief ornament of the State Dining Room is the French bronze-doré centerpiece ordered by Monroe in 1817. Fully extended, its seven mirrored sections are thirteen and a half feet long. Sixteen graceful Bacchantes complete the centerpiece and are used to hold fruit or candles.

To replace the two Monroe mantelpieces that were moved to the Red and Green rooms in 1902 a mantelpiece with carved buffalo heads was installed. The present mantel is a duplicate of the original, which was removed by Harry S Truman to his memorial library in Independence, Missouri. Above it is a compelling portrait of Abraham Lincoln by George P. A. Healy. The public tour of the White House ends at this point; visitors depart by the front door.

The **Family Dining Room,** which is not open to the public, contains examples of early nineteenth-century American Sheraton furniture. Since 1961, when an additional dining room was created on the second floor, it has been used primarily for small official breakfasts and luncheons and only rarely by members of the First Family for private dining.

The second floor of the White House was a jumble of private rooms and offices until the construction of the west or executive wing in 1902, with space for offices, conference rooms, facilities for the press corps, and a Cabinet room. The President's famous **Oval Office,** overlooking the Rose Garden, was added in 1909. Each occupant has decorated the office with his personal choices in furniture, paintings, and ornaments. Only the presidential seal, set into the ceiling, and the flags of the United States, the President, and the Armed Services remain constant.

The public is not admitted to the second floor, which is divided into two parts: the private living quarters of the President and his family at the west end and a suite of guest rooms on the east.

The **Lincoln Bedroom** is the only room in the Executive Mansion dedicated to a single President. Its somewhat somber Victorian furnishings readily evoke the spirit of the tormented Civil War leader. Lincoln signed the Emancipation Proclamation in this room, which served as his office and Cabinet room, never as his bedroom. With the adjacent sitting room, it is used as a guest suite for distinguished male visitors.

The intricately carved rosewood bed that dominates the room was purchased during Lincoln's administration as were the sofa and some of the chairs. Among the Lincoln memorabilia in the bedroom are a desk he used, books he read, and the only holograph copy of the Gettysburg Address signed and dated by the President.

More cheerful is the **Queens' Bedroom,** exuberantly decorated in shades of rose and white. Spacious and comfortable, the room has been used by such high-ranking female guests as Wilhelmina and Juliana of the Netherlands, Frederika of Greece, and Elizabeth II of Great Britain. In the room is an ornamental eighteenth-century overmantel mirror that Elizabeth presented to the White House during a visit in 1951, when she was still a princess. Adjoining the Queens' Bedroom is a small sitting room furnished in American and French Empire decor.

The nearby **Treaty Room** functioned as the executive Cabinet room from 1865 to 1902. In 1962 it was redecorated by Mrs. Kennedy as a sturdy Victorian sitting room with its original table, sofa, swivel chair, and clock. The room's ornate crystal chandelier was ordered for the East Room by Ulysses S. Grant. The green brushed-velvet wallpaper has a pattern copied from the room in which Lincoln died. On the walls are facsimiles of treaties that may have been signed in the room and a famous Healy painting, *The Peacemakers,* portraying Lincoln and his war generals. John Kennedy revived the room's traditional role by signing the Nuclear Test Ban Treaty there in 1963.

Beyond two pairs of sliding doors is the private apartment of the Chief Executive and his family—the Yellow Oval Room, furnished with many important American paintings and French Louis XVI furniture, and used as a reception room for visiting heads of state and other foreign guests; the President's Dining Room, with nineteenth-century French wallpaper depicting scenes from the American Revolution; a kitchen and pantry; four bedroom suites for the President, his wife, and their children; and the informal west sitting hall, with huge arched windows. On the third floor of the White House, enlarged during the administration of Calvin Coolidge, are a large solarium and seven additional rooms for staff and personal guests of the First Family.

Acknowledgments and Picture Credits

The Editors make grateful acknowledgment for the use of excerpted material from the following works:

"A Letter from a Self-Made Diplomat to His Constituents" by Will Rogers. Copyright 1927 by Curtis Publishing Company. The excerpt appearing on pages 153–54 is reproduced by permission of the Rogers Company and *The Saturday Evening Post.*

A Rose for Mrs. Lincoln by Dawn Langley Simmons. Copyright 1970 by Dawn Langley Simmons. The excerpt appearing on page 54 is reproduced by permission of Beacon Press.

A Thousand Days by Arthur Schlesinger, Jr. Copyright 1965 by Arthur M. Schlesinger, Jr. The excerpt appearing on pages 155–57 is reproduced by permission of the Houghton Mifflin Company.

A White House Diary by Lady Bird Johnson. Copyright 1970 by Claudia T. Johnson. The excerpt appearing on pages 158–59 is reproduced by permission of Holt, Rinehart and Winston, Inc.

Abigail Adams by Janet Whitney. Copyright 1947 by Janet Whitney. The excerpts appearing on pages 20 and 22 are reproduced by permission of Atlantic-Little, Brown.

Abraham Lincoln by Benjamin Thomas. Copyright 1952 by Benjamin Thomas. The excerpt appearing on page 49 is reproduced by permission of Alfred A. Knopf, Inc.

Carp's Washington by Frank Carpenter. Arranged and edited by Frances Carpenter Huntington. Copyright 1960 by Frances Carpenter Huntington. The excerpt appearing on page 76 is reproduced by permission of McGraw-Hill Book Company.

FDR by Roger Butterfield. Copyright 1963 by American Broadcasting Company Merchandising, Inc. The excerpt appearing on page 111 is reproduced by permission of Harper & Row, Publishers, Inc.

Forty-Two Years in the White House by Irwin Hood Hoover. Copyright 1934 by Irwin Hood Hoover; renewed 1952 by James Osborn Hoover. The excerpts appearing on pages 106–7 and 149–50 are reproduced by permission of the Houghton Mifflin Company.

In the Days of My Father General Grant by Jesse R. Grant, in collaboration with Henry Francis Granger. Copyright 1925 by Harper & Row, Publishers, Inc.; renewed 1953 by Nell Grant Cronan and Chapman Grant. The excerpt appearing on pages 144–46 is reproduced by permission of Harper & Row, Publishers, Inc.

John F. Kennedy, President by Hugh Sidey. Copyright 1963 by Hugh Sidey. The excerpt appearing on page 126 is reproduced by permission of Atheneum.

Lincoln and the Civil War in the Diaries and Letters of John Hay. Edited by Tyler Dennett. Copyright 1939 by Dodd, Mead & Company, Inc.; renewed 1967 by Tyler E. Dennett. The excerpt appearing on pages 141–43 is reproduced by permission of Dodd, Mead & Company, Inc.

Mandate for Change by Dwight D. Eisenhower. Copyright 1963 by Dwight D. Eisenhower. The excerpt appearing on page 133 is reproduced by permission of Doubleday & Company, Inc.

My Memoir by Edith B. Wilson. Copyright 1938, 1939 by Edith B. Wilson. The excerpt appearing on pages 151–53 is reproduced by permission of the Bobbs-Merrill Co.

Priscilla Cooper Tyler and the American Scene by Elizabeth Tyler Coleman. Copyright 1955 by the University of Alabama Press. The excerpt appearing on pages 140–41 is reproduced by permission of the University of Alabama Press.

Recollections of Full Years by Helen H. Taft. Copyright 1914 by Dodd, Mead Co. The excerpt appearing on pages 147–48 is reproduced by permission of Helen Taft Manning and Dodd, Mead Co.

This I Remember by Eleanor Roosevelt. Copyright 1949 by Anna Eleanor Roosevelt. The excerpts appearing on pages 107, 110–11, and 114 are reproduced by permission of Harper & Row Publishers, Inc.

Washington By-line by Bess Furman. Copyright 1949 by Bess Furman. The excerpt appearing on page 104 is reproduced by permission of Alfred A. Knopf, Inc.

When the Cheering Stopped by Gene Smith. Copyright 1964 by Gene Smith. The excerpt appearing on page 101 is reproduced by permission of William Morrow & Co., Inc.

The White House and Its Thirty-five Families by Amy LaFollette Jensen. Copyright 1958, 1962, 1965 by Amy LaFollette Jensen. The excerpts appearing on pages 28, 33, and 38 are reproduced by permission of McGraw-Hill Book Company.

The Editors would like to express their particular appreciation to Clement E. Conger, Curator of the White House, for his advice and cooperation in the production of this volume, and to Hillory A. Tolson, Executive Director of the White House Historical Association, for his invaluable assistance in obtaining pictorial material. The captions for this book were written by Thomas Froncek. In addition, the Editors would like to thank the following organizations and individuals:

Library of Congress, Prints and Photographs Division — Virginia Daiker, Leroy Bellamy
National Geographic Society, Washington, D.C.
White House Curator's Office — Carol Heinsius, Betty Monkman, Wilma Sands
White House Press Office — Ollie Atkins, Karl Schumacher
Lynn Seiffer, New York
Lynne H. Brown, New York

The title or description of each picture appears after the page number (boldface), followed by its location. Photographic credits appear in parentheses. The following abbreviations are used:

1886. LC 77 top, James Monroe clock in Blue Room; bottom, Blue Room. Both: WHHA 78 McKinley bedroom in White House. LC 79 Ida McKinley, 1900. LC 80 top, Cartoon from *The Verdict* January 1, 1900. New York Public Library; bottom, Detail from *Charge of the Rough Riders* by Frederic Remington, 1898. Remington Art Museum, Ogdensburg, New York 81 William McKinley by F. B. Johnston, 1901, (C)

CHAPTER V 83 Presidential portraits. BEP 84 center, Edith Roosevelt by Theobald Chartran. WHHA; clockwise, Theodore and Edith Roosevelt's sons, 1902. LC 86 Theodore Roosevelt's picture letter to Ethel Roosevelt, 1904. *Theodore Roosevelt's Letters to His Children,* Charles Scribner's Sons 87 Theodore Roosevelt, 1910. LC 88–89 East Room. WHHA 90 Engraving of wedding of Alice Roosevelt, 1906. LC 91 Front page news articles from *The New York Times,* October 19 and 20, 1901. 92 Program for state dinner given by Theodore Roosevelt, 1902. Theodore Roosevelt Collection, Harvard College Library 92–93 Engraving of state dinner given by Theodore Roosevelt, from *Harper's Weekly,* March 15, 1902. NYHS 94 left, Cartoon from *Puck,* 1906; right, William Howard Taft bathtub. Both: (C) 95 Woodrow Wilson and William Howard Taft in inaugural parade, 1913. Chicago Historical Society 96 Portrait of Woodrow Wilson by Sir William Orpen, 1919. WHHA 97 Portrait of Ellen Wilson and her three daughters by Robert Vonnah, 1913. Woodrow Wilson House 98 left, Woodrow Wilson and Edith Galt, 1915. LC; right, Woodrow Wilson and wife, Edith, after his stroke. Harris and Ewing 99 Sheep grazing on the White House lawn during World War I. LC 100 Ex-President Woodrow Wilson on the steps of his home on S Street. Harris and Ewing 101 Woodrow Wilson and wife, Edith, in an open carriage, 1921. LC

CHAPTER VI 103 Presidential portraits. BEP 104 Warren Harding lying in state in the East Room, 1923. LC 105 left, Portrait of Grace Coolidge by Howard Chandler Christy. WHHA; right, Calvin Coolidge with Sioux chiefs, 1925. LC 106–7 left, Herbert Hoover's favorite cartoon. Underwood & Underwood; center, Bonus Marchers in Washington, 1932. (C); right, General Douglas MacArthur and Major Dwight D. Eisenhower at Bonus riot, 1932. (Brown Brothers) 108 Franklin D. Roosevelt, 1939. (WW) 109 Cartoon from *Esquire* November 1938. American Heritage Publishing Co., Inc. 110 left, Cartoon from *Augusta Chronicle,* April 28, 1940. Franklin D. Roosevelt Library; right, Eleanor Roosevelt serving soup to unemployed women, 1932; center, Franklin and Eleanor Roosevelt, 1934. Both: (WW); bottom, Eleanor Roosevelt visiting war workers, 1943. LC 111 Franklin D. Roosevelt campaign buttons, 1940. (C) 112 Portrait of Eleanor Roosevelt by Douglas Chandor, 1949. WHHA 113 Queen Elizabeth and Eleanor Roosevelt in Washington, 1939. (UPI) 114 Yalta Conference, 1945. Franklin D. Roosevelt Library 115 Funeral of Franklin D. Roosevelt, 1945. (UPI)

CHAPTER VII 117 Presidential portraits. BEP 118–19 Renovation of the White House, 1950–52. All: National Archives 120 President Dwight D. Eisenhower and his grandchildren with Vice President Richard M. Nixon and his daughters, 1957. Dwight D. Eisenhower Library 121 top, *Deserted Farm* by Dwight D. Eisenhower, 1959. Dwight D. Eisenhower Library; bottom, Dwight D. Eisenhower practicing his golf swing on the White House lawn, 1953. (UPI) 122 John F. Kennedy in the Oval Office, 1963. John F. Kennedy Library 123 President and Jacqueline Kennedy with Pablo Casals in the East Room, 1961. John F. Kennedy Library 124 top left, Treaty Room. WHHA; bottom, Diplomatic Reception Room. WHHA; right, Portrait of Jacqueline Kennedy by Aaron Shikler, 1970. WHHA 125 Red Room. WHPO 126 John F. Kennedy lying in state in the East Room, 1963. John F. Kennedy Library 127 Funeral procession of John F. Kennedy, 1963. (Lee Battaglia) 128 top, Lyndon B. Johnson with Díaz Ordaz in the Yellow Oval Room, 1967. LBJ Library; bottom, Green Room. WHPO 129 Anti-Vietnam War pickets in front of the White House, 1967. (WW) 130 Oval Office. WHHA 131 The Richard Nixons with their two daughters and David Eisenhower in the second-floor dining room of the White House. WHPO 132 Presidential seal. WHPO 134–35 White House in the spring. WHPO

WHITE HOUSE MEMORIES 136 Drawing of the proposed floor plan of the White House by Benjamin Latrobe, 1807. LC 138–39 George Washington inaugural buttons, 1788. Smithsonian Institution 140–41 left, Invitation to Andrew Jackson's ball, 1828. Smithsonian Institution; right, Campaign ribbon of the Whig party, 1840. LC; bottom, Log cabin spoon, 1840. Smithsonian Institution 142 Henry Clay campaign ribbon, 1944. 143 James K. Polk campaign ribbon, 1944. 144 top, Zachary Taylor stove, 1848; bottom, campaign ribbon, 1860. 145 Homemade Abraham Lincoln leather ribbon, 1860. 146 top. Mourning ribbon for James Garfield, 1881; bottom, Mourning ribbon for Ulysses S. Grant, 1885. 148–49 top, Benjamin Harrison campaign plate, 1888; center, Benjamin Harrison pipe, 1888; William McKinley walking stick head, 1896. 150 top, Alton B. Parker and H. G. Davis campaign button, 1904; center, Benjamin Harrison and Levi P. Morton campaign button, 1888; bottom, Theodore Roosevelt and Charles W. Fairbanks campaign button, 1904. 151 Theodore Roosevelt campaign badge, 1904. 152 Uncle Sam hat bank, 1908. 154 Woodrow Wilson bandana, 1916. 155 Warren Harding nose-thumber, 1920. 156 Franklin D. Roosevelt wall clock, 1932. 157 Official inaugural program, 1933. 158–59 top, Donkey-elephant campaign toy, 1952; bottom, Eisenhower-Nixon campaign bucket, 1952. 160 top, John F. Kennedy campaign hat, 1960; bottom, Richard Nixon campaign ribbon, 1960. Memorabilia on pages **142–60;** Smithsonian Institution.

REFERENCE 166 Floor plan of the White House by Francis & Shaw, Inc.

Selected Bibliography

Aikman, Lonnelle. *The Living White House.* Washington, D.C.: White House Historical Association, 1970.

Carpenter, Frances, ed. *Carp's Washington.* New York: McGraw Hill Book Co., 1960.

Cunliffe, Marcus. *The American Heritage History of the Presidency.* New York: American Heritage Publishing Co., 1968.

Green, Constance McLaughlin. *Washington: Village and Capital, 1800–1878.* Princeton, N.J.: Princeton University Press, 1962.

Hurd, Charles. *The White House Story.* New York: Hawthorn Books Inc., 1966.

Jensen, Amy LaFollette. *The White House and Its Thirty-Five Families.* New York: McGraw-Hill Book Co., 1971.

Leish, Kenneth W., ed. *The American Heritage Pictorial History of the Presidents of the United States.* New York: American Heritage Publishing Co., 1968.

Pearce, Mrs. John N., *et al. The White House: An Historic Guide.* Washington: White House Historical Association, 1971.

Poore, Ben Perley. *Perley's Reminiscences of 60 Years in the National Metropolis.* Philadelphia: Hubbard Bros., 1886.

Singleton, Esther. *The Story of the White House.* New York: McClure Co., 1907.

Wolff, Perry. *A Tour of the White House with Mrs. John F. Kennedy.* Garden City, N.Y.: Doubleday & Co., 1962.

Index